Liam

May 2014

Rome.

"I ask that you pray to the Lord that he might bless me: the prayer of the people, seeking God's blessing for their bishop. In silence, please pray over me. . . ."

A Call to Serve

THE INSIDE STORY OF POPE FRANCIS

WHO HE IS, HOW HE LIVES, WHAT HE ASKS

Stefan von Kempis   Philip F. Lawler

SPCK

Dedication

For all my children, their spouses, and my grandchildren – Philip F. Lawler

For Marta, Stefan, and Maximilian, and for my godchildren
Jakob, Adrian and Ferdinand – Stefan von Kempis

Originally published in the United States of America in 2013
as *A Call to Serve: Pope Francis and the Catholic Future* by
The Crossroad Publishing Company, New York,
in cooperation with Verlag Herder, Freiburg, and
Libreria Editrice Vaticana

First published in Great Britain in 2013

Society for Promoting Christian Knowledge
36 Causton Street
London SW1P 4ST
www.spckpublishing.co.uk

British Library Cataloguing-in-Publication Data
A catalogue record for this book is available from the British Library

ISBN 978–0–281–07146–3

1 3 5 7 9 10 8 6 4 2

Printed in Great Britain by Ashford Colour Press

Produced on paper from sustainable forests

Contents

White Smoke over St. Peter's Square

A Bolt from the Blue

Entering the Conclave

The Bishop from the Ends of the Earth

Series of Surprises

Challenges

Preface: A Grand Invitation

The world was caught by surprise when a quiet Argentine, Jorge Mario Bergoglio, was introduced as the new leader of the Catholic Church. Humble in nature, quiet in style, he had not been among the journalists' *papabili*. His election was not what the Catholic world expected. But was it what the Church needed? The 1978 conclave chose a vigorous young Slavic Pope, ideally suited to expose the emptiness of Communist ideology. When he died, the Communist empire had crumbled—in no small part because of him. In 2005, one of the most brilliant scholars in papal history was elected to challenge secular intellectuals, showing that faith and reason are natural partners, not enemies.

Popes John Paul II and Benedict XVI were brilliant teachers and leaders for their times. But as they gathered in early March to choose the next Roman pontiff, the cardinals were not looking for a younger version of either man. The new Pope might not have the charisma of John Paul II or the intellect of Benedict XVI; who does? The cardinals were looking for a man with different talents for different times.

According to multiple reports, in 2005 many cardinals favored Cardinal Bergoglio. Eight years later, Cardinal Bergoglio's qualities stood out even more clearly.

Secular commentators see a papal election as a political contest, where candidates are rivals, with sharply contrasting policies. That approach is fundamentally misguided, and always produces confusion. When they enter the conclave the cardinals spend most of their time in prayer, not politicking. Prelates invariably report that the experience was like that of a silent retreat. Cardinal Timothy Dolan said that choosing a Pope boils down to a spiritual quest: "You look for a man who reminds you of Jesus."

Cardinal Bergoglio was not Ratzinger's rival in 2005, nor the opponent of the *papabili* in March 2013. When he was elected, he did not set out to undo the work of his predecessor; he simply brought his own approach, thoughts, and personality to the same work. St. Peter's successors come and go, but their job is always the same.

So it is absurd, for instance, to suppose that by choosing simpler vestments and a simpler residence, Pope Francis was implicitly rebuking his predecessor. Pope Benedict wore the beautiful vestments out of respect for the traditions of the office he had inherited. Pope Francis decided not to wear them in deference to public perceptions. Neither man was guided by a sense of personal style, much less vainglory; both were humbly seeking to serve the good of the Church.

The first post-conciliar pontiff

Every true Church reform is a return to some ancient source of spiritual strength. Vatican II was not a break from the centuries-old traditions of Catholic teaching, as Pope Benedict repeatedly stressed. Rather, the Council fathers drew attention to some older understandings of the faith that had slipped out of focus by the mid-20th century.

For 35 years—through the long pontificates of John Paul II and his trusted colleague Benedict XVI—the universal Church has profited from the teaching of popes who participated in Vatican II, and were determined to see its teachings implemented. Now the Church has the first Pope ordained after the opening of the Council, whose entire ministry has been guided by its vision of renewal.

Pope Francis no longer needs to explain the teachings of the Council. That work has been admirably done by his two predecessors, who have left a body of teaching that will take many years to digest. The challenge now is to put the teaching into practice. Vatican II proclaimed the "age of the laity," and reminded the faithful that all Catholics share equally in the responsibility to proclaim the faith. It falls to Pope Francis to rally the faithful in that great effort. One might almost say that John Paul II and Benedict XVI wrote the textbook on Vatican II, and Francis is producing the "how-to" manual. It is no coincidence that in Buenos Aires, then-Cardinal Bergoglio took the lead in recruiting lay Catholics as evangelists in their own right.

A Pope for the New World

Today there are more Catholics in Latin America than in Europe, and the growth of the Church is as robust in Africa as it is anemic in old "Christendom." So it is fitting that the Church of the New World is now providing infusions of strength and energy to the Old. African countries are now sending missionary priests to Europe and North America, repaying the countries whose missionaries first brought them the Faith.

The Diocese of Rome now has a bishop from Argentina. But this demographic shift also highlights new problems. The poverty and hunger that plague the southern hemisphere force the Church to confront the pressing realities of dire human need. The comfortable Catholics of Europe and North America might feel that they can afford to spend their energies debating, but in the global Catholic Church of the 21st century, millions of their brothers and sisters lack food, housing, education, and medical care. A Church that remains faithful to Jesus Christ cannot ignore those needs. And the new Pope has devoted much of his ministry to serving the poor in the slums of South America, urging his flock to do the same.

Still, Pope Francis persistently reminds us that the command of Christ is not only to serve the material needs of the poor, but also – even more importantly – to recognize their spiritual needs. When pressed to explain His public ministry, Jesus replied "Go and tell John what you hear and see: the blind receive their sight and the lame walk, lepers are cleansed and the deaf hear, the dead are raised up, and the poor have the Good News preached to them." [Mt 11:5] The preaching of the Gospel, the Lord indicated, was as great a gift as any physical miracle. In his first homily as pope, Francis told the cardinals who elected him that "we can build many things, but if we do not witness to Jesus Christ then it doesn't matter. We might become a philanthropic NGO but we wouldn't be the Church, the Bride of the Lord."

Is it more important for the Church to preach the Gospel of Christ or to serve the needs of the poor? That's a false dichotomy: there is no real distinction. Those who try to imitate Christ will do what Jesus did. Their preaching will be their service, and their service their preaching. The Church, Pope Francis has often said, is an instrument of Christ's work on earth. He spoke of a poor widow to whom he had offered some much-needed help and counsel:

"She told me: 'Father, I can't believe it; you make me feel important.' I replied, 'But lady, where do I come in? It's Jesus who makes you feel important.'"

A Pope for the New Evangelization

During his first days as Pope, Francis spoke time and again about the importance of rejecting a worldly, inward-looking, or "self-referential" view of the Church. The energies of the Church must always be directed outward, to bring the message of Christ to all nations. The Church is not an organization for Catholics, a private club serving its members. That attitude is horribly wrong, the Pope warns us: first because the Church belongs to Christ, not to the hierarchy; and second because the mission of the Church is to "make disciples of all nations." A Church that only serves its own members would betray its own purpose, and Christ.

The opposite of a "self-referential" Church would be a Church that constantly looks outward toward the world, alert for every opportunity to serve others, to bring Christ to those in need. It would be engaged in the New Evangelization that Pope Benedict declared as the great mission of our time.

The Church never stands still. If the faith is not advancing, it is probably in retreat. Many Catholics were undoubtedly looking for a pontiff who would defend the Catholic Church against attacks in an increasingly hostile world. But at its best the Church does not waste time defending itself, any more than Jesus did. When the life of the Church is service, the faith flourishes, even in adversity. An active Church grows even under persecution. The message of Jesus is always attractive, Pope Francis says, because it speaks to the depth of the human heart. If the Church preaches that message boldly and persistently, the faith will flourish.

Philip F. Lawler

Stefan von Kempis is an editor of Vatican Radio. He is the author of several books on Pope Benedict XVI, and editor of the monthly magazine Believing Together (Gemeinsam Glauben). He holds degrees in history, theology, and Islamic Studies, and lives in Rome with his family.

Philip F. Lawler is founder and editor of Catholic World News (CWNews.com). He had previously served as editor of Crisis magazine, the Boston Pilot, and Catholic World Report. Lawler is the author of six books on political and religious topics. His essays, book reviews, and editorial columns have appeared in newspapers around the United States and abroad.

White Smoke over St. Peter's Square

No one had really known what to expect from the conclave of March 2013, and yet the outcome was still a surprise. For the first time in over 1200 years a non-European was elected to the throne of St. Peter. Cardinal Jorge Mario Bergoglio of Buenos Aires was the first Jesuit ever to become Roman pontiff, and the first from the New World. The list of "firsts" lengthened when the new Pope chose the name "Francis," indicating that he would model his pontificate after the beloved St. Francis of Assisi.

The new Pope introduced himself to the world in the simplest terms, saying *"Buona sera"* ("Good evening") to the crowd of 200,000 people waiting in St. Peter's Square. He described himself as "a bishop from the ends of the earth," and asked the crowd to pray with him. Then in another unprecedented move—and under nearly comical circumstances— he placed a phone call to his predecessor.

A seagull perched atop the chimney on the roof of the Sistine Chapel.

Smoke from the Sistine Chapel chimney is visible over the statues lining the colonnade of St. Peter's Square.

The Seagull on the Roof

On Wednesday afternoon, March 13, tens of thousands of people stood in St. Peter's Square, umbrellas over their heads, watching a seagull. As the afternoon wore on, more and more people crowded into the Square; security officials only glanced quickly at their bags as the lines of new arrivals lengthened. Inside the Square, giant video screens set up along the Bernini colonnade showed the magnified image of a seagull, sitting quietly on a chimney high above the crowd. "That's an omen," someone said mysteriously.

The chimney was on the roof of the Sistine Chapel, where the cardinals were gathered in conclave to choose a successor to Pope Benedict XVI. From that very chimney, black smoke had billowed earlier in the day, signaling to the world that the cardinals' votes that morning had failed to produce a new pontiff. When a new Pope was chosen, white smoke from that same chimney would be the world's first public notice.

But no one really expected white smoke on Wednesday. It was still too early. The 115 cardinal-electors had only been locked into the Sistine Chapel (whose measurements are said to correspond exactly to those of the ancient Temple in Jerusalem) on Tuesday afternoon. By Wednesday evening they would have taken only five ballots. The consensus among Vatican journalists was that there was no clear frontrunner among the *papabili*, the prelates regarded as likely candidates for the papacy, so it would probably take many more ballots before the electors settled on one man.

White smoke signals the election of the new pontiff.

With no way to know what was happening in the Sistine Chapel, and no real expectation that a new pontiff would be named that Wednesday evening, the crowd at the Vatican settled for a much less satisfying spectacle—watching a seagull peck idly around the iron cap on the chimney.

Shortly after 7 p.m. the seagull flew away. The skies over Rome had already darkened, but powerful floodlights illuminated the roof of the Sistine Chapel. Then suddenly there were a few wisps of smoke: at first gray, but then unmistakably white. A cry went up from the crowd in St. Peter's Square. Bells began to ring. An infectious excitement quickly spread across Rome, and thousands of people began rushing to the Vatican to join the increasingly noisy, restive crowd waiting to greet the new Pope.

For Catholics it is a great joy to know that a new Pope has been elected. The celebration begins as soon as the white smoke appears, long before the new pontiff's name is announced. After an uneasy period of fatherlessness, the faithful welcome the news that there is another Vicar of Christ: another rock on whom the Church can build.

But who would it be? The celebration had already begun, yet the mystery remained. The world knew that a new Pope had been chosen, just over a month after Benedict XVI had announced his decision to resign. But only

The first, almost shy appearance on the balcony reveals more about the new Pope than words can say.

8:10 pm: crowds erupt in rejoicing as Pope Francis steps onto the middle loggia.

the cardinal-electors knew the identity of the man who would soon appear on the central balcony of St. Peter's Basilica.

The excitement grew as the Swiss Guard marched into St. Peter's Square in their distinctive uniforms designed by Michelangelo, carrying their ceremonial halberds. Two marching bands followed, assembled in front of the basilica, and played the Vatican and Italian anthems. Many in the crowd joined in singing the Italian anthem; others waved flags and chanted slogans. The day's steady rainfall had eased into a light drizzle.

Finally, about an hour after the white smoke had appeared, lights were turned on in the room behind the central balcony of St. Peter's. A few minutes later the senior cardinal-deacon, Jean-Louis Tauran, appeared on the balcony to make

the long-awaited announcement: *"Habemus Papam!"* ("We have a pope!").

Using the time-honored formula for the announcement, Cardinal Tauran went on to name the new pontiff: *Eminentissimum ac reverendissimum Dominum* (the most eminent and reverend lord): Georgium Marium. At this point confusion reigned over St. Peter's Square. What had he said? The cardinal, obviously caught up in the emotions of the moment, had rushed the words together, and echoes from the sound system made it difficult to hear the separate syllables. Most onlookers had expected to hear the name "Angelum" or "Odilum"—announcing that the conclave had chosen Cardinal Angelo Scola of Milan or Cardinal Odilo Scherer of Sao Paulo, the two most likely candidates in the eyes of the Vatican-watching journalists. "Georgium Marium"

was unexpected, and consequently the name was more difficult to discern.

"Georgium Marianum Bergoglio", and a storm of flashing smartphones unleashed.

Cardinal Tauran took a breath and continued with the formula, announcing that the newly elected Pope was of course *Sanctae Romanae Ecclesiae Cardinalem*—a cardinal of the Roman Catholic Church—and finally reached his surname: Bergoglio!

Now applause broke out, especially from the handful of native Argentines sprinkled through the crowd in St. Peter's Square. Yet at the same time there was a sense of confusion, almost approaching disbelief. Cardinal Bergoglio had not been ranked high on the list of *papabili*. He might have been seen as a compromise candidate, whose name could be brought forward when the leading contenders failed to capture the required two-thirds majority among the cardinal-electors. But this election had happened too quickly to allow for that explanation. Quite apparently, the cardinals gathered in the prayerful atmosphere of the Sistine Chapel had seen something in this humble Argentine prelate that the Vatican-watchers had not seen.

As they scrambled to learn something more about the new pontiff, Catholics quickly began to realize how dramatic his election had been. The first Jesuit, the first pope from Latin America: these distinctions were sensational enough. Then as a fuller picture emerged, it became clear that this Pope would bring a very new style of governance to the apostolic palace. He was known not for his speeches or his books, but for his very

simple style of life. As the archbishop of one of the largest cities in the Western hemisphere, Cardinal Bergoglio had still lived in a small apartment, cooked his own dinners, and rode the bus to his office.

A nd still there was another surprise coming, and another indication that the new Pope would stir things up at the Vatican. Cardinal Tauran finished his historic announcement by saying that the Pope had chosen the name: Franciscum. By selecting that name, the Pope was sending two powerful messages.

F irst, he was taking an entirely new name. Since the time of Pope Lando, who ruled the Church from 913 to 914, every Roman pontiff in the historical records has a Roman numeral after his name.

"Brothers and Sisters, good evening."
Pope Francis's simplicity surprises people around the world.

The only pope who chose an entirely new name, now known as John Paul I, explicitly said that he was taking the names of the two pontiffs who preceded him, John XXIII and Paul VI. When he chose a new name, Pope Francis showed a willingness to strike out in new directions.

S econd, he was invoking the memory of a 13th-century saint known for his embrace of radical poverty and his childhood love for all creation. St. Francis of Assisi is among the most beloved of all Catholic saints, and when the name "Franciscum" was announced, the immediate response in St. Peter's Square was jubilant. The

Joyful Catholics
from East Asia.

A tiny witness to
a great event.

Beaming compatriots of the new pope.

world often pictures St. Francis after the
fashion of a famous mosaic in the church
dedicated to him in Assisi, showing the
saint preaching to the birds. (Maybe that
seagull on the roof of the Sistine Chapel
had a premonition?) But the impulsive,
unrestrained joy of St. Francis is not easily
reconciled with the quiet, careful traditions of Vatican governance. Pope Paul
VI had once sighed, "In this Vatican there
will never be a Pope Francis. Because St.
Francis destroyed the man-made rules;
he just wanted to follow the Gospel."

"Buona sera."

In Rome there are no more exciting
moments than the times when a newly
elected Pope makes his first appearance
on the loggia of St. Peter's Basilica. The
people in St. Peter's Square are anxious,

curious. The Pope is, in the first place,
the Bishop of Rome; will the faithful of
Rome accept him? The first impression
that the new Pope makes when he meets
the public—often at a time of turbulence,
amid conflicting expectations—can set
the tone for an entire pontificate.

The cardinals who had just elected
Pope Francis were well aware of the drama
that was unfolding. Many of them took
places on the side balconies of St. Peter,
from which they would be able to see both
the new Pope and the crowd below. Cardinal
Angelo Scola—once regarded as the likeli-
est choice of this conclave—was spotted

"I thank you for your welcome."

public with a quick wave of his right hand. He wore a simple white cassock, without the traditional purple cape, the *mozzetta*, customarily worn by a Pope on such occasions. Around his neck was a pectoral cross made of iron, not gold. Closer inspection would reveal that the cross showed an image of Jesus as the Good Shepherd, carrying across his shoulders the lost sheep of the Gospel parable. Mildly plump (if not as rotund as Pope John XXIII), he showed the world a quiet smile, a good-natured face, large ears, and old-fashioned glasses.

His first appearance prompted applause and shouts of "Francesco." But the noise soon died down. Pope Francis let his hands drop down and simply stood, silently, smiling down on the people in St. Peter's Square. This was to be his emblematic first moment: a Pope who communicated without words, radiating his love out across the city and the world but saying and doing nothing to create a scene.

A native of Argentina, Pope Francis had doubtless seen how populist leaders like Juan Perón and Cristina Kirchner drew attention to themselves, playing in the limelight on the balcony of the Casa Rosada, the presidential mansion in Buenos Aires. He wanted no spectacle of that sort. A fellow Jesuit later remarked, "He knows exactly what he's doing. Just standing there doing nothing, and in this way he brings everything down."

on the side balcony, as was Cardinal Oscar Rodriguez Maradiaga of Tegucigalpa, Honduras, who had been touted as a candidate to become the first Latin American Pope in the days before the conclave of 2005. The faces of the cardinal-electors showed their emotion, as well as their fatigue. Later in the evening, when those cardinals had their first free time since the opening of the conclave, a few walked around St. Peter's Square and chatted with reporters. Without exception they seemed exhausted after days of intense and prayerful concentration on their most crucial task.

Finally, at 8:10 pm Pope Francis appeared on the central loggia and saluted the

"Brothers and sisters, good evening to you," he said at last, in Italian. *"Buona sera,"* the first public words of his pontificate, are said quietly, without any special emotional inflection or grand gestures. Those words closed a chapter in the history of the papacy: a chapter that began when Pope Benedict XVI, in his final public appearance before his resignation took effect, ended an address to the crowd at the papal summer residence in Castel Gandolfo by saying, with the same simplicity, *"Buona notte"*—"Good night."

"You know, it was the duty of the conclave to give Rome a bishop," the new Pope continued:

"It seems, my brothers, the cardinals have gone almost to the ends of the earth to find him. But here we are. I thank you for this reception. The Diocese of Rome now has its bishop. Thank you!"

The new bishop of Rome asks the faithful for their prayers.

Thus began the pontificate of the first pontiff from the New World: with a simple "good evening" and a self-deprecatory reference to his origin in a distant land. (Older Romans could recall how Pope John Paul II won over the crowd at his own first appearance, by admitting that his Italian was not fluent and saying, "If I'm wrong you will have to correct me.") Pope Francis had immediately established an impression of confident simplicity. Significantly he referred to himself as the "Bishop of Rome," never using the term "Pope" in this first address.

> "We share many common goals—from the promotion of peace, social justice and human rights, to the eradication of poverty and hunger—all core elements of sustainable development."
>
> *Ban Ki-moon,*
> *Secretary General of the United Nations*

The bishop and his people

After these opening words Pope Francis waited until the applause died down, then continued: "I would like first to say a prayer for our Bishop Emeritus Benedict XVI. Let us all pray together for him, that the Lord bless him and the Mother of God protect him." With that he led the people in St. Peter's Square in the most familiar prayers that all Catholics know: an Our Father, Hail Mary, and Glory Be. Not far away, in the Alban Hills south of Rome, the former Pope was watching his successor's address on television at Castel Gandolfo.

Everything about this first papal appearance was unique, suggestive of an entirely new approach to the papacy. Pope Francis began his work as the 265th successor to St. Peter not by making a grand gesture of announcing a sweeping reform, but by leading the people of Rome in prayer. "And now we start this way, bishop and people, the way of the Church of Rome, which presides in charity over all the churches," the Pope continued: "Let us always pray for one another. Let us pray for the whole world, that there may be a great spirit of fraternity. It is my hope for you that this journey of the Church, which we start today, and in which my Cardinal Vicar, here present, will assist me, will be fruitful for the evangelization of this most beautiful city."

> "And now, we take up this journey: Bishop and People. This journey of the Church of Rome which presides in charity over all the Churches. A journey of fraternity, of love, of trust among us. Let us always pray for one another. Let us pray for the whole world, that there may be a great spirit of fraternity."
>
> *Pope Francis*

The faithful in St. Peter's Square wait quietly to greet the new Pope.

By referring to the "bishop and people" as a team, the Pope was affirming the vision of the Second Vatican Council, which emphasized the common baptismal calling of all Christians and saw the Church as the "People of God." There was also a slight Latin American flavor to his words, since the Church in that region has done so much since Vatican II to be a genuine Church of the people, especially promoting the "preferential option for the poor" that was endorsed by the Latin American bishops at a historic meeting in Puebla, Mexico, in 1979—with Father Jorge Mario Bergoglio among those in attendance.

Young people from Argentina cheer as they hear the news that the Church has chosen the first pope from their native land.

When he said that the Church in Rome "presides in charity," the Pope was reckoning back to the way St. Ignatius of Antioch described the primacy of Rome in the early days of Christianity. The formula has been given greater emphasis by Catholic leaders since Vatican II, because it expresses the case for papal primacy in a way that does not raise objections from other Christian churches. By mentioning the presence of the vicar-general of Rome, Cardinal Agostino Vallini, Pope Francis was making it clear that he will take quite seriously his position as bishop of the city. He is, as he introduced himself, the Bishop of Rome; any other claim to authority flows from that fact.

Finally, in those first few words from the balcony of the Vatican basilica, Pope Francis had sounded the call to evangelization. He thereby underlined his commitment to continue and perhaps even expand the "New Evangelization" that had been energetically promoted by Popes John Paul II and Benedict XVI before him. The same missionary zeal to spread the Gospel through the world can also be found in the life story of his model, St. Francis of Assisi, who set out for the Holy Land in 1219 determined to introduce the Sultan Saladin to the Christian faith.

That short introductory speech by Pope Francis was not, it turns out, quite as simple as it seemed. In fact it was a neatly organized message, containing clear indications of the pontiff's thinking and his plans. Still the new Pope was not quite finished surprising his people.

A new Pope is expected to deliver his solemn blessing, the *Urbi et Orbi*

blessing, to the city and the world.
But Francis announced:

"Before the Bishop blesses his people,
I ask you to pray to the Lord to bless
me: the prayer of the people asking
the blessing for their Bishop."

With that the Pope bowed deeply
toward St. Peter's Square. Here was
something entirely new: a Pope asking
the people for their blessing. Many of
the people in St. Peter's Square, caught
entirely off guard by the request, simply stared confusedly at the giant video
screens. The cardinals on the side balconies of St. Peter's were puzzled. With the
speakers of the sound system turned out
toward the crowd, they could not hear the
Pope's words. A few days later Cardinal
Angelo Comastri disclosed: "When we
saw that the people suddenly began to
pray silently, we asked each other: 'What
happened? Why is it suddenly so quiet?'"

The Pope then donned a stole and
read the solemn blessing, tracing the sign
of the cross over the city of Rome and by
extension over all the world—even the
distant corner of the world from which he
had been called to serve as Vicar of Christ.

After the blessing, Pope Francis ended
his audience with a few closing words:

"Pray for me and we will see one another soon! Tomorrow I want to go to
pray to the Madonna, that she may protect Rome. Good night and sleep well."

As he turned to go back into the
basilica, he said one more word, which
the microphones did not pick up.
It sounded like *"Ciao."*

"He will surprise us all."

That very evening, despite the cardinals'
solemn vows to preserve the secrecy of the
conclave, stories began to emerge—usually from unnamed sources, of uncertain
reliability—about how the election had
unfolded. According to one report, Cardinal
Bergoglio had been the leading vote-getter

"As a champion of the poor and the most
vulnerable among us, he carries forth
the message of love and compassion that
has inspired the world for more than
two thousand years—that in each other
we see the face of God. As the first pope
from the Americas, his selection also
speaks to the strength and vitality of a
region that is increasingly shaping our
world, and alongside millions of Hispa-
nic Americans, those of us in the United
States share the joy of this historic day."

U.S. President Barack and Michelle Obama

from the first ballot on Tuesday; other reports contradicted this account, saying that
his total had risen gradually. On the decisive fifth ballot, when it became clear that
Cardinal Bergoglio would reach the necessary 77 votes, the electors reportedly burst
into applause. But the newly elected pontiff
had a different reaction, according to re-

The new Pope prepares to don the stole, symbolic of his office, before delivering his first blessing.

ports; he said to his fellow cardinals: "God forgive you for what you have done today."

At a meeting with reporters after the election, Cardinal Karl Lehmann of Mainz, Germany acknowledged that Cardinal Bergoglio had not seemed a leading candidate before the conclave, because "there was not as much talk about him as about others." But he said that during the meetings of cardinals in the days preceding the conclave, the "general congregations," the Argentine cardinal began to emerge as a force to be reckoned with. "Just in the last two or three days," he said, "one could feel, even in the way he spoke, that power behind it." Cologne's Cardinal Joachim Meisner also admitted that he was not terribly well acquainted with the prelate from Buenos Aires. But he expressed great confidence in the new Pope. "He will surprise us all," he predicted.

Actually, the surprises had already begun. Immediately after his election, Pope Francis had felt the desire to call his predecessor, Benedict XVI. But that would not be an easy desire to realize. To ensure the secrecy of the conclave, technicians had removed all phone lines and jammed all electronic signals. They had done their job well; no phones worked in the Sistine Chapel.

One alert Vatican Radio employee had a solution. There was a working phone in a room above the balcony of St. Peter's: a room that radio broadcasters used when they were doing live commentary on papal Masses. A few Vatican Radio employees had used the room the previous day, as a base for covering the beginning of the conclave. In order to avoid interfering with the cardinals, they had taken a roundabout route: up a freight elevator to the colonnades, then up an iron spiral staircase to reach the remote room in St. Peter's. The room was crowded with stacked chairs and equipment, but the telephone did work. Pope Francis was not deterred by the messy room, which no pontiff had ever before visited. He sat at the table that a radio technician had used, and placed a call to Castel Gandolfo.

Unfortunately Benedict XVI, who was watching the events from the Vatican on television with his aides, did not hear his phone ringing. Only after a series of messages, relayed through intermediaries, did the historic conversation actually take place. Reporters were later told that Francis and Benedict had exchanged warm greetings and agreed to a face-to-face meeting in the near future. The Vatican press office did not reveal that the Pope had placed his call from a cluttered workroom.

The disarmingly informal style of the new Pope continued to confound the expectations of seasoned Vatican officials during these first few hours after his election. After his appearance on the loggia, a limousine was waiting to take him to the Domus Sanctae Marthae, the residence where the cardinals had stayed during the conclave, for a dinner with the cardinal-electors. But the Pope apparently never noticed the waiting car. The next day Cardinal Timothy Dolan of New York told reporters what had happened next. The cardinals had arrived by bus at the Vatican residence, he said, and were waiting for the car to deliver the Pope, when "the last bus pulls up, and guess who gets off the bus? Pope Francis." Brazilian cardinals who accompanied him on that bus ride took a few blurry photos, capturing the image of the Pope sitting quietly in front of his old friend, Cardinal Clàudio Hummes.

The easy informality of Pope Francis was a marked contrast with the style of his predecessor, Benedict XVI, who had carefully observed protocol and invariably wore the "correct" vestments for a Roman pontiff. That contrast caused some misunderstanding and gave rise to some inaccurate reports of early tensions inside the Vatican. Msgr. Guido Marini, the master of ceremonies for papal liturgies, had repeatedly tried to put the purple cloak, the *mozzetta*, across the Pope's shoulders before his first appearance on the loggia. According to one rumor, Pope Francis finally lost patience and snapped: "The carnival is over." The rumor was false; eyewitnesses said that the Pope actually explained politely that "I would prefer not to" wear the *mozzetta*. If there were some people who saw the simplicity of Francis as a reason to mock the formality of Benedict, the Pope himself was not among them.

The New World Pope

Still it was impossible not to notice how different Pope Francis was—not only from his immediate predecessor, but from every pontiff in recent memory. The differences began with his nationality. It had been 1,272 years since the last non-European, the Syrian St. Gregory III, had occupied Peter's throne. And of course there had never before been a pope from the Western hemisphere. Hundreds of newspaper headlines hailed Francis as the "New World Pope."

I n Argentina, it was 3 p.m.—siesta time—when the white smoke arose from the Sistine Chapel. President Cristina Kirchner was delivering a speech at an exhibition center on the outskirts of Buenos Aires when the news arrived that Cardinal Bergoglio had been chosen. The Argentine leader's relations with Cardinal Bergoglio had frequently been contentious. In one recent, memorable confrontation, after the cardinal criticized a proposal to allow same-sex couples to adopt children, Kirchner had complained that his views were reminiscent of "medieval times and the Inquisition." Now Kirchner continued with her prepared text and only added a few words of congratulations at the end of her address. Some members of the audience whistled, indicated their distaste for her lukewarm reaction to the historic news. Only later, in the evening, would Kirchner's office send a short congratulatory telegram, expressing "appreciation and respect" for the prelate with whom the Argentine president had often clashed.

A rgentina's parliament did not interrupt its proceedings—a series of talks honoring the recently deceased Venezuelan President Hugo Chàvez—when the news arrived. The state television network did not break from its regular programming. But among the people at large the news had an electrifying effect. People began gathering in the Plaza de Mayo, the central square in Buenos Aires

Celebrations on the streets of Rome as the new Pope is introduced.

known for political demonstrations, carrying their nation's blue-and-white flags and chanting "Argentina, Argentina" or "Francisco, Francisco." Motorists joined in the celebration with a chorus of automobile horns. The soccer star Lionel Messi announced that he wanted to dedicate the 2014 World Cup to the new Pope.

In the slums of Buenos Aires, residents were deeply moved by the election of their countryman. "Bergoglio's one of us; he often visited here," said one resident. Others pointed to a garage that had served as a makeshift church for immigrants from Paraguay. There, they said, the cardinal celebrated Mass, "then he spoke with us and ate *locro* [a soup of corn and meat] with us." In the parish office, under a corrugated tin roof, a young mother recalled how the cardinal had stepped off a bus to celebrate Mass for her son's First Communion. The visits by "Padre Jorge" had brought some change to the neighborhood, where violence, disease, and poverty are rife. More important, they had brought some love: some clear indication that the Church cared about the poor. Now the residents of the slum celebrated the fact that their favorite prelate had been named leader of the universal Church.

"As the rabbi of the Fundación Judaica, I can say that Pope Francis and I have had a beautiful relationship and I'm really happy for him. He speaks with sensitivity and humility."

Rabbi Avruj of Buenos Aires

A Jesuit and a Franciscan

The election of history's first Jesuit Pope would have been historic in itself. A new Pope's choice to be known as "Francis" would have been historic as well. But the conjunction of the two—the fact that the first Jesuit pope chose to be named after the founder of a different religious order—caused a sensation in the Catholic world. Was Pope Francis a Jesuit or a Franciscan at heart?

The Jesuits arose in the 16th century as the spearhead of the Catholic Counter-Reformation, and developed a reputation for intellectual rigor and unswerving loyalty to Rome. The Franciscans, on the other hand, emerged in the 13th century out of a commitment to radical poverty and simplicity. The Jesuits were organized along military lines and respectful of authority; the Franciscans thrived on spontaneity rather than structure. Jesuits amassed enormous public influence by acting as teachers at the great universities and chaplains at the great courts, while Franciscans worked with the poor and promoted simple devotions rather than academic theology.

Yet through history the two famous religious orders were similar in their mis-

sionary outreach, and there were remarkable similarities between their founding fathers. Both St. Francis of Assisi and, 300 years later, St. Ignatius of Loyola traveled to the Holy Land. Both sought a renewal in the Church, and meditated deeply on the Gospels, imagining themselves in the scenes of Christ's life. St. Ignatius taught this approach in his Spiritual Exercises; St. Francis had already put it into practice by introducing the Christmas crèche as a form of devotion.

This approach to the Gospel, imaginative yet practical, made a deep impression on Jorge Mario Bergoglio. At the opening of his book on spirituality, *Open Mind, Believing Heart*, he says:

"The apostolic zeal is nourished by the contemplation of Jesus Christ, as he walked, as he preached, as he healed, as he looked at others. The heart of a priest must practice this contemplation and thereby solve the fundamental challenge of his life, namely his friendship with Jesus Christ."

No special treatment: After the conclave the new Pope takes his seat on the bus with the cardinals who elected him.

It was while reading the poems of St. Francis that Ignatius was "struck by lightning" and realized his mission. "St. Francis was our founder's model," said the Italian Jesuit Father Antonio Spadaro, of the prestigious Jesuit journal *Civilta Cattolica*.

For Father Spadaro, the 30 seconds of silence while the new Pope looked down from St. Peter's balcony on the crowd on the plaza, spoke volumes about the attitude of the new pontiff. "He does not want any attention for himself, but he wants to put God at the center," said Father Spadaro. "That's how we Jesuits are."

Jesuits are comprehensively educated, prepared to take important roles in the Church. But each member of the Society of Jesus promises not to seek major of-

At St. Patrick's cathedral in New York, some of the faithful react emotionally to the new Pope's appearance.

fice or personal advancement. Members of the order swear allegiance to the Pope, vowing to be available for any mission at the pontiff's direction. "Jesuits are supposed to obey the Pope, not become Pope," says Father Spadaro. "For us this is a new, initially frightening situation."

To complicate matters still further, there are tensions within the Society of Jesus. As provincial of the order in Argentina, Father Jorge Mario Bergoglio became the focus of those tensions; he was sharply criticized by some of his fellow Jesuits for being too rigid in his devotion to Catholic orthodoxy, too slow to embrace social activism. His fellow Jesuits declined to renew Father Bergoglio's term as provincial. Jesuits are often controversial. Father Bergoglio was a controversial Jesuit. Yet now he will be, for millions of people around the world, the public face of the Jesuit order.

When the new Pope was introduced, passersby did not hear champagne corks popping at the Gesù, the Jesuit headquarters near the Vatican. The doors were not open to welcome the public to a celebration. The façade of the building stood as quiet and aloof as ever, with only a halo of light in a window here and there. Father Paul Mankowski, a Jesuit biblical scholar in Chicago, believes that by choosing the name "Francis," the new Pope was sending a message to the Catholic world in general and his own Jesuit order in particular: a call to renew the "radical and universal call to follow Jesus." Father Mankowski added: "He also is fully aware that it was a Franciscan,

2nd-grade students in Mrs. MacLean's class at St. Paul's Catholic school in Valparaiso, Indiana, watch the news of the Pope's election.

Indian sand artist Sudarshan Pattnaik finishes his portrait of the new Pope Francis.

Pope Clement XIV, that suppressed the Society of Jesus. . . . I don't mean that his choice of name is a threat, but we all heard him chamber a cartridge, so to speak."

The Italian philosopher Massimo Cacciari saw the arrival of Pope Francis in very different terms, suggesting that when a Jesuit Pope called himself by the name Francis, he was pointing to internal peace among Christians: "It is as if all at once true peace has broken out in the Church. The Jesuit loyalty to the pure doctrine is combined with the caritas of the Friars Minor; the soldier Ignatius meets the beggar of God." Still, he remarked, it would be "no small undertaking to combine the Escorial with the Portiuncula"—comparing the baroque palace of King Philip II in the Spanish Sierra, where Jesuits once held sway, with the tiny chapel where St. Francis of Assisi is buried. Cacciari decided: "I cannot predict the outcome, but we certainly will not be bored."

A woman in Hyderabad, Pakistan, shows that although she is far from Rome, she is close to the new Pope.

Goodbyes: the last ride on the popemobile during the audience on February 27, 2013.

A Bolt from the Blue

According to reports that leaked into the public domain after the papal conclave of 2005, Cardinal Joseph Ratzinger had led in the voting from the start, but after a few ballots he was still short of the required two-thirds majority. His ascent to the papacy was assured when the prelate who stood second in the voting, Cardinal Jorge Mario Bergoglio, indicated his support for the German cardinal, who would become Pope Benedict XVI. Nearly eight years later the roles were reversed. Pope Benedict, with his stunning resignation from the papal ministry, cleared the way for the election of Cardinal Bergoglio.

When Pope Benedict announced his plan to resign, at a meeting with cardinals on February 11, 2013, it came—in the words of Cardinal Angelo Sodano, dean of the College of Cardinals—"like a bolt from the blue." No one had expected this. Even Vatican officials who worked closely with the pontiff on a daily basis had not been taken into his confidence. As if to illustrate Cardinal Sodano's point, a few hours after the historic announcement, the dome of St. Peter's Basilica was struck by lightning as a thunderstorm swept across Rome.

February 11 was expected to be a quiet Monday at the Vatican. The cardinals who were present in Rome gathered in the apostolic palace for an "ordinary consistory," a meeting at which the Pope

February 11, 2013. Benedict XVI announces his resignation at a consistory of cardinals.

would announce plans for the canonization of several new saints. At first the meeting went just as anticipated: the Pope and the cardinals prayed together, the names of the prospective saints were read aloud. But exactly 33 minutes into the meeting, Pope Benedict disclosed to his "dear brethren" that he had another reason for calling them together that day: "to communicate a decision of great importance for the life of the Church."

Reading in Latin from a prepared text, the Pope revealed: "After having repeatedly examined my conscience before God, I have come to the certainty that my strengths, due to an advanced age, are no longer suited to an adequate exercise of the Petrine ministry."

As his stunned listeners struggled to understand his words, the Pope continued:

"I am well aware that this ministry, due to its essential spiritual nature, must be carried out not only with words and deeds, but no less with prayer and suffering. However, in today's world, subject to so many rapid changes and shaken by questions of deep relevance for the life of faith, in order to govern the barque of Saint Peter and proclaim the Gospel, strength of both mind and body are necessary, strength which in the last few months, has deterio-

rated in me to the extent that I have had to recognize my incapacity to adequately fulfill the ministry entrusted to me.

"For this reason, and well aware of the seriousness of this act, with full freedom I declare that I renounce the ministry of Bishop of Rome, Successor of Saint Peter, entrusted to me by the Cardinals on 19 April 2005, in such a way, that as from 28 February 2013, at 20:00 hours, the See of Rome, the See of Saint Peter, will be vacant and a Conclave to elect the new

After announcing his plan to resign on February 11, 2013, Benedict XVI leaves the consistory—and leaves the cardinals with a great deal to discuss.

Supreme Pontiff will have to be convoked by those whose competence it is."

Pope Benedict concluded his brief statement by thanking those who had assisted him during his pontificate, asking the intercession of the Virgin Mary to guide those who would choose his successor, and saying that "I wish to devotedly serve the Holy Church of God in the future through a life dedicated to prayer."

A small crew from the Vatican Television Center, CTV, was on hand for the consistory, recording the event as the center records most papal appearances. The images that CTV soon sent out to the world showed the faces of the cardinals registering first incomprehension, then dismay as the gravity of the Pope's statement sunk in. Pope Benedict himself, however, appeared perfectly calm as he announced that, "with full freedom," he would become the first Roman pontiff in nearly 600 years to renounce the chair of St. Peter.

"At first we were all stunned and surprised," said Cardinal Walter Kasper, the retired president of the Pontifical Council for Christian Unity, who was among those present for the papal announcement. "There was a silence; we initially did not say anything." But then came "a mood like an earthquake." An audio recording by Vatican Radio captured the audible shock, followed by a buzz of excitement as many cardinals began speaking at once.

A decision made over time

Cardinal Kasper allowed that at dinner with the Pope just a few days earlier, he had noticed the 85-year-old pontiff's frailty. But even if the Pope was "very thin and fragile," the cardinal never imagined that he would resign. A papal resignation seemed unthinkable.

But was it really so surprising? Pope Benedict had dropped several hints that he might consider it. As far back as 2010, in a lengthy interview, he had stated clearly that a Roman pontiff could indeed resign, and might even have a moral obligation to do so, if he could no longer exercise his duties adequately. He had made a special effort to pray at the grave of the hermit-Pope, St. Celestine V, who at the close of the 13th century had been the last Roman pontiff to resign his office. During a trip to the earthquake-ravaged town of L'Aquila in the Abruzzo Mountains in 2009, Pope Benedict had laid his *pallium* —the vestment symbolizing a bishop's office—on the glass coffin of St. Celestine. And quite frequently, in his sermons and public statements, the German Pope had insisted that the Church is led by Christ himself, while he, the Pope, was only another Christian trying to serve the Lord.

Eight years earlier Pope Benedict had begun his pontificate by describing himself to the crowd in St. Peter's Square as "a simple and humble worker in the Lord's vineyards." He spoke frequently about his admiration for Blessed John Paul II, and at times it seemed that Benedict thought of himself as a mere caretaker in the papacy: a bland figure especially in comparison with his charismatic predecessor. Benedict did not have a natural gift for speaking to large crowds. He did not have the strength or the inclination to undertake great pastoral voyages. He was visibly uncomfortable with excessive applause (especially during Mass) and with photo sessions. He went about his business carefully, methodically, even lovingly, but without grand gestures.

(Curiously, when he became Pope in 2005, Benedict XVI did not give up the apartment in Rome where he had lived for years. Only in 2012 did he finally pass it along to Archbishop Gerhard Ludwig Müller, whom he had appointed to his own old post as prefect of the Congregation for the Doctrine of the Faith. Might he have been thinking from the start of his pontificate that he could eventually retire to live in that apartment?)

If Pope Benedict had contemplated retirement as an abstract possibility in 2005 or even in 2010, the ensuing years would certainly have sharpened his thinking, as old age began to take its physical toll. Arthritis had made him increasingly

A lightning bolt strikes St. Peter's Basilica on February 11, 2013, the very day on which Pope Benedict XVI announced his resignation.

hesitant in his gait, unsteady on his feet. He had begun walking with a cane, and using a wheeled platform, rolled by aides, to cover the long central aisle of St. Peter's Basilica for papal liturgies. He needed more frequent pauses for rest during the day. After a trip to Mexico and Cuba in the spring of 2012, doctors had told him that he should not attempt a trans-Atlantic voyage again. It was at about that time, according to Msgr. Georg Ratzinger, the Pope's older brother, that the pontiff began leaning toward resignation. Shortly after he announced his plan to step down, the Vatican disclosed that a projected encyclical on faith, which he had reportedly begun drafting the previous summer, would not be completed. It was telling that this prolific author, who had produced dozens of books and scores of scholarly articles, no longer had the stamina to complete an encyclical letter.

Yet Pope Benedict had continued to keep a demanding schedule. At 85 he was working at a pace that would challenge much younger men. There was no evidence at all that the Pope was losing his mental acuity. A few days after his shocking announcement, at a meeting with priests of the Rome diocese, the Pope apologized for not having a prepared address, and then launched into a cogent, well organized, and perceptive 45-minute extemporaneous talk on the interpretation of Vatican II. Still, Pope Benedict, who was probably his own toughest critic, felt that his powers were diminished. In his resignation he suggested that the papacy faced challenges that would require the energies of a younger man.

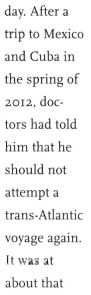

Is it possible then to imagine a situation in which you consider a resignation by the Pope appropriate? "Yes. If a Pope clearly recognizes that he is no longer physically, psychologically, and spiritually capable of handling the duties of his office, then he has the right and, under some circumstances, also an obligation to resign."

Pope Benedict XVI in an interview with Peter Seewald in Light of the World

Crises and responses

Pope Benedict XVI will certainly be known to church historians as the first modern pontiff to resign. But what else will historians write about him?

This scholarly pontiff from Bavaria had never wanted to succeed his illustrious friend Pope John Paul II. In fact he had twice sought to resign from his post in the Roman Curia, hoping to return to academic life; he stayed on at the Polish

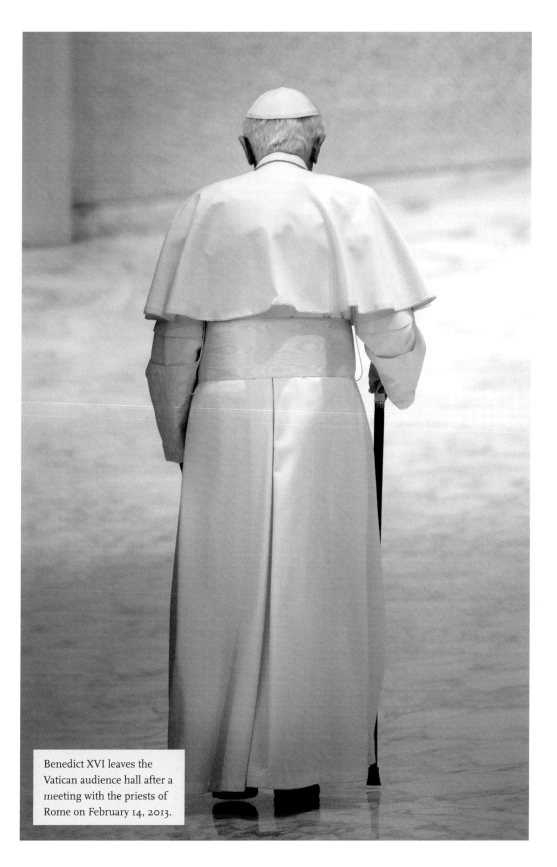

Benedict XVI leaves the Vatican audience hall after a meeting with the priests of Rome on February 14, 2013.

The Vatican spokesman, Father Federico Lombardi, faced a torrent of questions about the resignation.

Islamic world with his famous speech at Regensburg in 2006, and for lifting the excommunication of a traditionalist bishop who turned out to be (unbeknownst to the Pope) a Holocaust denier. He was assigned blame for the sex-abuse scandals that broke out across Europe during his pontificate—although the crimes had been committed long before he was in office, and he had set tough new standards for dealing with offending priests and with bishops tainted by the scandals. Finally there was the "Vatileaks" affair, in which confidential papal correspondence was made public, and the leaks were eventually traced to the Pope's own valet.

Without doubt there had been public-relations gaffes during his pontificate, and the machinery of the Vatican had not run smoothly. Pope Benedict was not an outstanding administrator. He admitted these deficiencies without hesitation. Yet the Pope did not deserve the blame for all the problems that arose during his reign. Still he chose not to fight back against his critics. In early January 2013, in a sermon preached in the Vatican basilica, he reflected that "bravery consists not in lashing out aggressively, but in enduring a beating and in standing up against prevailing opinions." In an era marked by rising hostility to Christianity, he said, "we will also be beaten by those who oppose the Gospel."

Pope's urging. After his election to the papacy, he spoke of his great admiration for Pope John Paul II, but said that the Church also needs "little popes, who give their own." With characteristic humility he placed himself in that category.

When Benedict announced his decision to step down, many reporters rushed to the conclusion that he was tacitly admitting the failure of his efforts as a pontiff. To be sure he had faced difficulties—even embarrassments—during his eight years as Pope. His harsher critics now portrayed the pontificate as a series of missteps. He was criticized for provoking anger in the

The Pope's critics often overlooked

Celestine V

1294 was a difficult year for the Catholic Church. For two years the Holy See had been vacant, and the 11 voting cardinals in the Perugia conclave could not agree on a new Bishop of Rome. Powerful Roman families were at odds with each other about the future of the pontificate, and Charles II of Anjou was exerting political pressure on the cardinals. To break the stalemate the cardinals turned to a hermit, Peter of Morrone, who had a reputation for sanctity. They apparently hoped that the new pontiff would reign for a short time—just long enough to allow the contending powers to regroup, form new alliances, and prepare for another papal election.

The hermit from the Abruzzo mountains thus received a message informing him that he had been chosen as the supreme pontiff. Although he knew his own inadequacies, and feared that he would be defenseless against the intrigues of the Roman Curia, Peter also felt obliged out of obedience to accept his election. He rode a donkey to his coronation—earning the sympathy of the public and the contempt of the cardinals. On August 29, 1294, Peter of Morrone became Pope Celestine V.

Just as he feared, the new Pope quickly fell prey to the machinations of powerful political cliques. His hope of ending the intrigues by withdrawing into private prayer proved fruitless. Before the year was out, he concluded that he could not rule effectively, and on December 13 he submitted his resignation to the cardinals. (Historians have been unable to determine with certainty whether his withdrawal was entirely voluntary.) His successor, Boniface VIII, placed him under house arrest to guard against the remote possibility that Celestine's supporters might return him to the papacy. So the retired monk died in exile in May 1296 at Castel Fumone. His pontificate lasted only five months and nine days.

St. Celestine V, who was Pope from July to December 1294, had been the last pontiff to resign. He was canonized in 1313. On 29 April 2009, Benedict XVI laid down his papal *pallium* on Celestine's burial shrine in L'Aquila.

Declaratio

Dear Brothers,

I have convoked you to this Consistory, not only for the three canonizations, but also to communicate to you a decision of great importance for the life of the Church. After having repeatedly examined my conscience before God, I have come to the certainty that my strengths, due to an advanced age, are no longer suited to an adequate exercise of the Petrine ministry. I am well aware that this ministry, due to its essential spiritual nature, must be carried out not only with words and deeds, but no less with prayer and suffering. However, in today's world, subject to so many rapid changes and shaken by questions of deep relevance for the life of faith, in order to govern the barque of Saint Peter and proclaim the Gospel, strength of both mind and body are necessary, strength which in the last few months, has deteriorated in me to the extent that I have had to recognize my incapacity to adequately fulfill the ministry entrusted to me. For this reason, and well aware of the seriousness of this act, with full freedom I declare that I renounce the ministry of Bishop of Rome, Successor of Saint Peter, entrusted to me by the Cardinals on 19 April 2005, in such a way, that as from 28 February 2013, at 20:00 hours, the See of Rome, the See of Saint Peter, will be vacant and a Conclave to elect the new Supreme Pontiff will have to be convoked by those whose competence it is.

Dear Brothers, I thank you most sincerely for all the love and work with which you have supported me in my ministry and I ask pardon for all my defects. And now, let us entrust the Holy Church to the care of Our Supreme Pastor, Our Lord Jesus Christ, and implore his holy Mother Mary, so that she may assist the Cardinal Fathers with her maternal solicitude, in electing a new Supreme Pontiff. With regard to myself, I wish to also devotedly serve the Holy Church of God in the future through a life dedicated to prayer.

From the Vatican, 10 February 2013
BENEDICTUS PP XVI

Benedictus PP XVI

the positive changes that he had brought to the Vatican. Even before his ascent to the papacy he had demanded vigorous action against priests who molested children—overcoming opposition from other leading prelates to set a tougher policy line. He had approved financial reforms to ensure transparency and to eliminate suspicions of money-laundering at the Vatican bank. He had taken special care to appoint able and apostolic new bishops. He had quietly pressed for the resignations of bishops who proved themselves incompetent or unworthy, and peremptorily removed a few who resisted the plea to resign.

Determined to promote beauty and a sense of transcendence in Catholic worship, Benedict XVI had encouraged widespread use of the traditional, Latin liturgy of the Roman Church (the "Extraordinary Form") and worked to restore a greater sense of reverence in the more common vernacular liturgy. He had created new ecclesiastical structures—ordinariates—to accommodate Anglicans who wished to return to union with the Holy See while preserving their own rich liturgical traditions. Under his guidance, a new English-language translation of the Mass was

"I have the greatest admiration for the Pope's gesture, for the courage, the spirit of freedom, and the great awareness of responsibility for his office."
Father Federico Lombardi, Vatican spokesman

approved, using more dignified language and showing greater respect for the literal meaning of the original Latin prayers.

Pope Benedict receives ashes at his last public Mass as pontiff on Ash Wednesday, February 13.

Believers from all over the world during the
last Angelus audience of Benedict XVI in
St. Peter's Square.

But above all Pope Benedict—perhaps
the most accomplished scholar to become
Pope in modern times—had been a teacher.
His first encyclical, *Deus Caritas Est (God
Is Love)*, set the tone for his later writings,
demonstrating his remarkable ability to put
lofty theological ideas into clear straightforward language. The encyclical also displayed
the German Pope's determination to challenge the secular world with the essential elements of Christian belief. "It is not an ethi-
cal choice of a lofty idea that inspires one to
become a Christian, but the encounter with
an event, a person, which gives life a new
horizon and a decisive direction," he wrote.

A scholar in the tradition of the early
Fathers, Benedict stood and fought for the
reconciliation of faith and reason, tirelessly
insisting that the two were not in conflict
but should be seen in cooperation. He
called for accurate doctrine combined with
simple faith; he wanted to preach orthodox

"The courage to engage the whole breadth
of reason, and not the denial of its gran-
deur—this is the program with which
a theology grounded in Biblical faith
enters into the debates of our time."

Benedict XVI in Regensburg

Catholic dogmas in undiluted form without sacrificing the willingness to engage in
open dialogue with skeptics and unbelievers. His greatest enemy, against which he

hammered away in his public addresses, was the "dictatorship of relativism"—the prohibition of all objective standards for truth and falsehood, right and wrong.

In the evening of February 28, as the papacy of Benedict XVI comes to an end, some of the faithful gathered in St. Peter's Square to accompany him with their prayers.

Searching for the God "with a human face"

Benedict saw, far more clearly than John Paul II, the limits and obstacles to honest dialogue with Islam. His famous speech at Regensburg was intended as a challenge to responsible Islamic leaders, asking them to take a stand in favor of reason and against violence. Yet it was this same Pope who established a new committee for Catholic-Islamic dialogue, stopped with a Muslim imam for a moment of silent prayer at the Blue Mosque in Istanbul, and encouraged Saudi King Abdullah to set up a center for inter-religious dialogue in Vienna.

Leaders of other Christian denominations did not have high hopes for ecumenical progress when Benedict became Pope. After all he was the principal author of *Dominus Iesus*, the document issued by his Congregation for the Doctrine of the Faith in 2000 that had referred to other Christian groups as "defective." Yet under his guid-

February 17, 2013: the faithful in St. Peter's Square bid farewell to Pope Benedict XVI.

concentrated on the essential message of the Christian faith: the belief in a God "with a human face," revealed in Jesus Christ. Without a belief in God, he warned, "humanity loses its orientation." Confident that honest thinkers would recognize the inherent desire to seek out the infinite and establish a relationship with the Almighty, he approved a new Vatican project, the "Courtyard of the Gentiles," in which Christians engaged in thoughtful exchanges with skeptics and unbelievers. He poured his energies into the "New Evangelization," a determined effort to revive interest in the Gospel in Western Europe and North America, societies where the Christian faith had once shaped social life, but had now fallen into desuetude.

ance the Vatican and the Lutheran World Federation reached a breakthrough agreement on a contentious matter of doctrine, issuing a Joint Declaration on Justification. The world's Orthodox leaders came to regard Pope Benedict as an ally. The Russian Orthodox hierarchy joined Benedict's fight against secularization in Europe, and relaxed the icy hostility that it had shown toward the Vatican under John Paul II. The Ecumenical Patriarch Bartholomew I of Constantinople, who was invited by Benedict to preach in the Sistine Chapel, became a good friend.

"Though I am now retiring to a life of prayer, I will always be close to all of you and I am sure all of you will be close to me, even though I remain hidden to the world."

Benedict XVI, February 14, 2013

Worried that the 21st-century world was not properly acquainted with Jesus Christ, Pope Benedict undertook a remarkable project: the 3-volume work *Jesus of Nazareth*, a bid to rescue an accurate portrayal of Jesus by correcting the excesses of the historical-critical method of Biblical analysis. He had planned the work for years, telling a Vatican Radio audience in 2002 that he hoped to write it after his retirement. When he became Pope, he

In his dealing with other religions and with the secular world, Pope Benedict made the decision to move forward with the project in his spare time. But he made it clear that he was writing as a theologian, expressing his own views, rather than as a pontiff speaking with the authority of his office. *Jesus of Nazareth* proved enormously successful, climbing the bestseller charts and giving the world an entirely new perspective on a Pope who taught as a scholar.

Differing reactions

Now this remarkable man, this brilliant scholar and humble leader, had announced his own voluntary departure. "I looked at the other cardinals and saw in their faces the same feelings: surprise, shock, dismay, grief," said Cardinal Paul Poupard. When Father Federico Lombardi, the papal spokesman, was bombarded with questions from reporters at a hastily arranged press conference that Monday afternoon, he revealed that he had not been prepared for the Pope's announcement. "I honestly do not know," he replied to several questions. The German daily *Frankfurter Allgemeine Zeitung* described the odd scene with the headline: "Papal explainer at a loss for an explanation."

Although the Pope had some physical problems, Father Lombardi assured reporters, there was "no acute disease" prompting his resignation; he "simply feels the burden of old age." Pope Benedict had undergone surgery recently, but it was only a routine replacement of the battery for a pacemaker that had been implanted years earlier. He

One more blessing for the faithful. Pope Benedict at his Angelus audience on February 17.

had suffered an injury to his head when he fell during his trip to Mexico in 2012, but the damage had not been severe. Yet the Pope had made the decision to resign long ago, Father Lombardi said; this was not a reaction to the "Vatileaks" scandal.

When reporters sought reactions from passersby in St. Peter's Square, some gave voice to their dismay. "We live in such troubled times, with so many crises," said one, "and now even the Pope gives up." From Krakow, Cardinal Stanislaw Dziwisz was quoted as saying: "Jesus doesn't come down from the Cross!" Those sounded like bitter words, coming from the prelate who had served for years as the private secretary to Pope John Paul II and had witnessed the Polish Pope's long, agonizing, and very public struggle with illness and death. The

Polish cardinal said that his words had been taken out of context, and insisted on his admiration for Pope Benedict. Yet then he gave an interview in which he paid an odd sort of compliment to the current Pope, saying that he admired Benedict "because he was always so closely associated with the late Pope John Paul, the greatest pope of the century!"

From around the world reactions of international leaders poured into the Vatican: from U.S. President Barack Obama, British Prime Minister David Cameron, German Chancellor Angela Merkel, French President Francois Hollande, and others. The message from Israeli President Shimon Peres was particularly powerful: "I deeply regret the Pope's stepping down. It is a singular decision, for he is a singular and courageous man." Peres referred to Pope Benedict as a "unique spiritual leader," and observed that "wisdom never grows old." The 137 Islamic scholars who had answered Benedict's call to dialogue after the Regensburg address said that his "graceful resignation" was "remarkable."

Some other reactions were not so favorable. New York's Cardinal Timothy Dolan admitted his confusion: "I want to know what's going on!" Berlin's Cardinal Rainer Maria Woekl said that he feared the Pope's retreat from public life had harmed the public image of the papacy. Cardinal George Pell of Sydney, Australia, said: "I

hope we are not entering an era when elected popes withdraw, one after another." He feared that anyone who opposed the policies of a future pontiff would begin lobbying for his resignation, undermining his authority. "The Pope from the land of the Reformation has revolutionized the papacy," wrote Daniel Deckers in the *Frankfurter Allgemeine Zeitung.* "It has become a temporary office." British philosopher Roger Scruton saw the resignation of Pope Benedict in connection with the recent resignation of the Archbishop of Canterbury, Dr. Rowan Williams; both, he said, were "thinkers, not fighters," and had "given way to the intimidation and pressure from militant laity, gay lobbies, and political correctness."

"A German pope who publicly thanked the people of the United Kingdom for winning the Battle of Britain was, clearly, a man with an unusual perspective on, and insight into, contemporary history."

George Weigel

Dr. Rowan Williams, the retired worldwide leader of the Anglican communion, had his own special perspective. He saw the Pope's decision as signaling a new understanding of the papacy: one that could spark greater ecumenical progress. The Anglican prelate said that the "de-mythologizing" of the papacy could be the most significant lasting effect of Pope Benedict's decision. The Pope, he told

Pope Emeritus

Once his retirement from the office of Bishop of Rome became official at 8 pm on February 28, Benedict XVI was no longer the Pope. Nor is he a cardinal, since his status as a member of the College of Cardinals lapsed in April 2005 when he became Pope. He remains a bishop, however. The pontificate is an elected office, which can be (and in this case was) resigned. A bishop is consecrated for life.

But what does one call a Pope who has resigned, to give him proper respect without creating confusion? Father Federico Lombardi, the Vatican spokesman, agreed that the question was a delicate one, which would take some careful thought to resolve. After several consultations about protocol and canon law, the Vatican announced that Benedict would be known as "Pope Emeritus," or alternatively "Emeritus Roman Pontiff."

The Code of Canon Law had made some provision for a papal resignation, but none for the title he would bear after he stepped down. But a diocesan bishop, after submitting his resignation upon reaching the age of 75, is generally known as the "Bishop Emeritus" of his diocese.

Benedict XVI is still addressed as "Your Holiness." He still wears a white cassock, but without the shoulder-length cape worn by the Roman pontiff. The Fisherman's Ring that he wore has been deliberately defaced so that it cannot function as an official seal. The official papers of his pontificate will be transferred to the Vatican Secret Archives, where they will presumably not be made accessible for 50 years.

In his retirement the Pope Emeritus will live in the Mater Ecclesiae residence, located between St. Peter's Basilica and the Vatican Gardens. The residence, which once served cloistered nuns, is being remodeled; Benedict is expected to move there—from his temporary residence at Castel Gandolfo—when the renovations are completed.

Pope Emeritus Benedict XVI. will live in the monastery Mater Ecclesiae between St. Peter's and the Vatican Gardens.

Pope Emeritus Benedict XVI has a lifelong love of classical music, and is known as a talented pianist. He has not said whether he plans to write any further scholarly works in his retirement. He left an encyclical on Faith unfinished when he left the papal throne.

St. Peter's Square could barely contain the crowd of people who came for the last general audience of Benedict XVI.

Vatican Radio, had shown that he was "not some kind of god-king who goes on 'til the end." Rather, he said, "He is the bishop who brings together, who mediates, who cares for the community of bishops."

A willing 'Prisoner of the Vatican'?

While the news of his resignation reverberated around the world, Pope Benedict himself seemed calm, unmoved by the excitement he had caused, freed of the burden he had been carrying. In public appearances he thanked the people for their support, saying that he felt "almost physically" the power of their prayers. On Ash Wednesday, when he celebrated the last public Mass of his pontificate, the congregation burst into lengthy applause just before the end of the ceremony. "Thank you," the Pope said gently, then added: "Now let us return to prayer."

"I am not returning to private life," Pope Benedict XVI said at his final general audience on February 27. Some commentators wrongly interpreted that phrase to mean that the Pope intended to remain a public figure, even after he stepped down the following evening.

"We Orthodox Christians will always honor him as a friend of our church."

Bartholomew I, Patriarch of Constantinople

The outgoing Pope knew that this would be impossible. A high-profile "Pope emeritus" would be a constant source of confusion for the Catholic world. Every sentence the former Pope uttered, every public gesture he made, would be scrutinized for signs of disagreement with the reigning pontiff. Having looked to Pope Benedict as an authoritative teacher, the faithful could not easily adjust to thinking of him as just another theologian. And yet it would be the new Pope, not the ex-Pope, who would hold teaching authority.

So what did the Pope mean when he said that he would not return to private life? He explained: "I am not returning to private life, to a life of trips, meetings, receptions, conferences, etc," he said. "I am not abandoning the Cross." What the Pope here meant by the "private life" was actually the life of a major public figure: a prominent individual who attends conferences and receptions, who travels and makes speeches. This is what Pope Benedict said he would not do. Instead he promised to devote himself entirely to prayer.

Pope Benedict explained his curious use of the term "private" in the course of his final Wednesday audience. He remarked that when a prelate accepts his election as Peter's successor, he gives up his own private life. "He belongs always and entirely to everyone, to the whole Church," Pope Benedict said. "His life, so to speak, is totally deprived of its private dimension." Thus when he said that he would not return to "private" life, the Pope was not contrasting "private" with "public" activity. Rather he was indicating that his life would not be his own "private" possession; he would remain totally dedicated to the service of the Church.

By resigning his Petrine ministry, Benedict XVI was voluntarily relinquish-

Farewell to the Apostolic Palace. Benedict XVI departs the Vatican by helicopter for Castel Gandolfo, February 28, 2013.

ing his power to control Vatican policies. He surely had his own fixed opinions on actions that should be taken, but he would

> "He will be missed as a
> spiritual leader to millions."
> *David Cameron, British Prime Minister*

no longer be able to take them. Yet as he explained to the crowd in St. Peter's Square that day, Pope Benedict firmly believed that he could now serve the Church best by his prayers. Back in July 2010, Pope Benedict had said that when St. Celestine resigned in 1294, that pontiff was not trying to avoid the challenges of ecclesiastical life; he was trying to respond to those challenges in the best way he knew, through contemplative prayer.

Unfortunately St. Celestine became a "prisoner of the Vatican" after his resigna-

tion—although he was not confined inside the Vatican walls. His successor, Pope Boniface VIII, fearing the confusion that a "Pope Emeritus" might cause, had St. Celestine arrested and confined in a castle, invisible to the world. Now Pope Benedict, who has followed St. Celestine into resignation, would imitate him in another respect, confining himself to an apartment inside the Vatican, doing his best to disappear from public life.

On February 28, at 8 pm Rome time, the resignation of Pope Benedict XVI officially took effect. The Pope shook hands with tearful aides as he left the ap-

The changing of the guard: at 8 pm on February 28, as the pontificate of Benedict XVI officially ended, the Swiss Guard closed the door to the papal residence at Castel Gandolfo and left their duty, since the Swiss Guard serves only the reigning Pope.

"I am simply a pilgrim beginning the last leg of his pilgrimage on this earth. But I would still—with my heart, with all my love, with my prayers, with my reflection, with all my inner strength—like to work for the common good and the good of the Church and the world."—Pope Benedict, speaking to the faithful gathered at Castel Gandolfo on February 28, just before his resignation took effect.

ostolic palace just before 5 pm and drove across the grounds of Vatican City to the heliport. As the helicopter lifted off, all the bells of the Vatican pealed. Hundreds of residents of Rome went to their rooftops to wave as Benedict passed overhead on the last trip of his pontificate. Bells rang out once again to greet him when he arrived at the papal summer residence in Castel Gandolfo, where he was formally greeted by a cadre of Church leaders and civic officials.

Soon after his arrival, Pope Benedict appeared at the balcony of the papal residence to speak briefly with the people who had congregated in the courtyard below. "I am simply a pilgrim beginning the last leg of his pilgrimage on earth," he said. While he was stepping down from the papacy, he assured the faithful that he would continue to devote himself entirely to supporting the Catholic Church "with my heart, with my love, with my prayers, with my reflection, and with all my inner strength."

At exactly 8 pm, the doors of the apostolic palace were closed, and the Swiss Guard detail left their post, since the Swiss Guard are responsible only for the personal safety of the reigning pontiff. (The Vatican gendarmerie will continue to provide security for the former Pope.) The papal apartments at the Vatican were sealed off, and the Fisherman's Ring worn by Benedict XVI was defaced so that it could never again be used as an official seal. The *sede vacante* period had begun.

The Sistine Chapel is closed to visitors as Vatican workers make preparations for the papal election.

Entering
the Conclave

Pope Benedict XVI had barely announced his resignation before Italian newspapers began printing lists of *papabili*: the prelates viewed as likely candidates for the papacy. The papers also speculated on the influence of "great electors"—powerful prelates who probably would not be candidates themselves, but could influence the votes of other cardinals. Cardinal Angelo Sodano, the longtime Secretary of State and still the dean of the College of Cardinals, loomed as a major force in the cardinals' deliberations—even though he, at the age of 85, was too old to take part in the conclave itself. His successor as Secretary of State, Cardinal Tarcisio Bertone, would also play an important role. Not only is the Secretary of State the most powerful man in the Vatican after the pontiff himself, but Cardinal Bertone was also the *camerlengo*, the official responsible for administering the immediate tasks of the Holy See in the absence of a Pope.

As soon as Pope Benedict's resignation took effect on February 28, the Holy See would officially be vacant; the *sede vacante* period would begin. Under the rules governing the process of papal succession, 15 days would have to pass—to allow cardinals from around the world time to reach Rome—before a conclave could begin. During that period, the cardinals who were present in Rome would govern the Church collectively, meeting each day in "general congregations" to discuss the needs of the Church and the qualities required for the next Pope.

In this case, unprecedented in the modern papacy, the *sede vacante* period did not begin with the death of a pontiff, but with the announcement of a resignation. So the days leading up to the conclave would not be given over to mourning. The process of choosing a new pope could begin even before the reigning pope left the scene. Thus the speculation began in earnest on February 11. Would the conclave elect a Pope from Italy (Angelo Scola of Milan? Gianfranco Ravasi, the president of the Pontifical Council for Culture? Angelo Bagnasco of Genoa, the president of the Italian bishops' conference?), or from elsewhere in Europe (Christoph Schönborn of Vienna, Peter Erdö of Budapest), or reach out to Africa (Peter Turkson, the Ghanian president of the Pontifical Council for Justice and Peace) or Asia (Luis Antonio Tagle, the exciting young Archbishop of Manila)? Several *papabili* from the New World appeared on the journalists' lists, most notably Odilo Scherer of Sao Paulo and Marc Ouellet, the former Archbishop of Quebec now serving as prefect of the Congregation for Bishops.

Even some cardinals joined in the public speculation that fueled the tota-papa: the papal lottery. Cardinal Francisco Coccopalmiero pointed to a possible Brazilian candidate, Cardinal Raymundo Damasceno Assis of Aparecida. Cardinal Donald Wuerl of Washington, DC, declared it unlikely that a cardinal from the U.S. would be selected, since any statement by an American pontiff would be scrutinized for political overtones. Cardinal Leonardo Sandri, an Argentine native with years of experience inside the Roman Curia, said that the Church is "ready for an African pope," but the world at large might not be. Campaign-style posters urging a vote for Cardinal Peter Turkson popped up on the streets of Rome—embarrassing the African cardinal, who had nothing to do with them. New names were mentioned frequently but carefully, to avoid the perception of open lobbying. Cardinal Karl Lehmann of Mainz, Germany, remarked: "You can only say that anyone whose name is dropped too often will meet with a certain amount of skepticism."

Cardinal George Pell of Sydney seemed inclined toward an Italian pontiff. "The pope is the Bishop of Rome," he said, "and I think it would not do well

to leave the Church without an Italian pope for so many years." For that reason, he told a journalist, the Italian cardinals would "enter the conclave with a slight advantage." But then he reversed himself, saying that "I would not exclude a foreign papal candidate, either." The Australian prelate added: "It would not surprise me if in the next 50 to 100 years several popes were elected from South America."

Newspapers produce their competing lists of *papabili*, listing the cardinals considered most likely to be elected Pope.

"Perhaps this will be a conclave of change," said Cardinal Paul Poupard. One change already seemed likely to guide the cardinals' thinking. Now that the possibility of a papal resignation had become a reality, it was logical—wasn't it?—to assume that the cardinals would choose a younger man, perhaps in his 60s, so that the Church would not face the probability of another conclave in just a few years' time.

There was no single obvious candidate for the papacy. For that matter it was impossible to whittle the list down to two or three leading *papabili*. In past conclaves there had sometimes been two main contenders, and the cardinals either chose one of them or settled on a compromise candidate. But in 2013 there were a dozen or more names on every list of *papabili*. Analysts agreed that the cardinals would probably take some time to winnow the field before settling on a new pontiff.

As the long pontificate of John Paul II came to its close, cardinals all around the world recognized that the Holy Father was approaching the end of his life, and had ample time to think about a suitable successor. Pope Benedict's resignation had caught them unprepared. The search for a successor was just beginning.

Before the conclave

There were 117 cardinals under the age of 80, and therefore eligible to vote in a papal election. But Cardinal Julius Darmaatmadja of Jakarta announced that illness would prevent him from traveling to Rome; and Cardinal Keith O'Brien of Edinburgh resigned amidst accusations of sexual impropriety, and said that he would give up his role in the conclave to avoid creating distractions. Cardinal Mahony of Los Angeles, who had been relieved of all public duties in that archdiocese because of his mishandling of the sex-abuse scandal, came to Rome despite an energetic online campaign to deny him a role in the conclave. So 115 electors would choose the next Pope.

The cardinal-electors entering the conclave would represent the most diverse such group in Church history. Never before had so many different nations sent cardinals to a papal election. For the first time an elector born in mainland China would cast a ballot in the Sistine Chapel: Cardinal John Tong Hon of Hong Kong. (Cardinal Luis Tagle of Manila had a Chinese mother as well.) Europeans were still over-represented, accounting for roughly half the voting cardinals, although Europeans comprise less than one-quarter of the world's Catholics. Italy, too, would be over-represented, with 28 cardinals—eight more than at the conclave of 2005. However, at this conclave, unlike previous papal elections, the number of non-Europeans would balance the European cardinals.

In the fall of 2012—perhaps already looking forward to the resignation that he would announce a few months later—Pope Benedict appointed the last group of cardinals of his pontificate. The consistory, in which he handed out six new red hats, was unusual in two respects. First, it was the second consistory of the year, suggesting

Italian Cardinal Angelo Sodano, the former Secretary of State, upon arrival for a general congregation at the Synod Hall in the Vatican, March 6, 2013.

Cardinal Tarcisio Bertone, in his role as *camerlengo*, is the interim caretaker of the Holy See during the *sede vacante* period. On the evening of February 28, after the resignation of Benedict XVI took effect, he seals off the papal apartments in the apostolic palace.

that the Pope felt he had left some business unfinished at the earlier conclave. Second, none of the new cardinals was European, and five of the six were from developing or emerging countries: a Lebanese, an Indian, a Nigerian, a Colombian, and a Filipino as well as a U.S. citizen. It appeared evident that Benedict was deliberately increasing the geographical diversity of the College of Cardinals.

"I ask you to remember me in prayer before God, and above all to pray for the cardinals, who are called to so weighty a task, and for the new successor of the apostle Peter: may the Lord accompany him with the light and strength of his Spirit."

Benedict XVI
at his last general audience on February 27, 2013.

Pope Benedict had tightened the rules for election, declaring that the next Pope must achieve a two-thirds majority among the electors: in this case, 77 votes. This new rule might mean a longer conclave, as a leading candidate slowly gained support. But it could also mean a strong mandate for the pontiff who was chosen. According to leaked reports from the conclave of 2005, Cardinal Joseph Ratzinger asked for another round of ballots after he had gained a majority, hoping for—and receiving—the two-thirds support that showed a clear confirmation of his leadership.

As Benedict's resignation date drew nearer, some cardinals began to question whether it was really necessary to have a full 15-day waiting period before beginning the conclave. After all, they reasoned, cardinals from other countries had ample time, after the Pope's announcement on February 11, to reach Rome by February 28, when the *sede vacante* period would begin. Especially since there would be no need to plan a papal funeral, the cardinals could begin their work of choosing a new pontiff immediately. A streamlined schedule would allow the cardinals to return to their own dioceses in time for Holy Week, and give the new pope time to prepare for the Easter Triduum in Rome.

But other cardinals, especially those far from Rome, argued against haste. They would need time to become acquainted with each other, they reasoned. Given the novelty of the situation and the importance of their choice, they should not rush their decision. A conclave scheduled too soon might actually have an unintended effect. Boston's Cardinal Sean O'Malley explained that "the conclave will be protracted if we do not have the time beforehand to talk with each other." Many of the arguments in favor of a quick conclave were advanced by cardinals working at the Vatican, and

U.S. Cardinals Donald Wuerl, Timothy Dolan, Francis George, and Roger Mahony leave the North American College to go to the Vatican's Domus Sanctae Marthae, the Vatican residence where the cardinals would stay during the conclave.

Sean Cardinal O'Malley in Rome in March 2013.

Timothy Cardinal Dolan arrives for the conclave.

Cardinal Gianfranco Ravasi of the Pontifical Cultural Council preached the traditional Lenten Retreat for the pope and his closest associates.

Cardinal Baselios Cleemis Thottunkal of India arrives at the Vatican on Thursday, March 7. Cardinals from around the world are gathered in Rome for general discussions prior to the opening of the conclave that would elect the next Roman pontiff.

Children play in the foreground as Cardinal Joseph Zen Ze-kiun, of Hong Kong, walks in St. Peter's Square following a meeting of the cardinals on Thursday, March 7, 2013.

much of the resistance came from cardinals outside Rome. Behind their reasoned arguments one could detect an unspoken refusal, on the part of the "outsiders," to be caught unawares if officials of the

> "I call as my witness Christ the Lord who will be my judge, that my vote is given to the one who before God I think should be elected."
>
> *The promise each cardinal recites as he casts his ballot in the conclave.*

Roman Curia put forward their favorite candidate for a quick confirmation.

Benedict's preference?

In any case, the 15-day waiting period was fixed in Church law; it could only be altered by Pope Benedict. Eight days before the

end of his pontificate, the papal spokesman Father Federico Lombardi disclosed that the pope was considering changes in the rules for a papal election. Those changes came on Monday, February 25, at the beginning of his last week in office. Pope Benedict's amendment to the regulations allowed the cardinals to establish an earlier date for the conclave, as long as all the eligible electors were present. At the same time he revised the penalties for any cardinal or Vatican official who violated the strict secrecy of the conclave; such an offense would not bring automatic excommunication.

If Pope Benedict had any preferences among the *papabili*, he was scrupulously silent about them. But his silence did not stop speculation. The pope had appointed Cardinal Angelo Scola, his old colleague on

Cardinal George Pell, of Australia, right, arrives for a Vespers celebration in St. Peter's Basilica, Wednesday, March 6, 2013.

Cardinals Odilo Scherer (l), and Geraldo Majella Agnelo (r), both of Brazil, arrive for a meeting on Saturday, March 9.

Chinese Cardinal John Tong Hon (l) leaves the Synod Hall on March 7.

Cardinal Theodore Adrien Sarr (l) and Cardinal Wilfrid Fox Napier of South Africa (r) arrive for the General Congregation at the Synod Hall on March 7.

the editorial board of the theological journal *Communio*, as Archbishop of Milan, the largest see in Europe—thus virtually assuring that the Italian prelate's name would appear high on any future list of *papabili*. It was a coincidence that the Pope met with Cardinal Scola, along with other bishops from the Lombard region, in one of his last private audiences; that meeting had been scheduled months earlier. But their appearance together sparked a final round of newspaper reports linking the two.

The Pope had also given Cardinal Gianfranco Ravasi a chance in the pre-conclave spotlight, appointing him to preach the Lenten Retreat at the Vatican. In one of his meditations, delivered while the Pope's decision to resign was still reverberating in the news, Ravasi compared the outgoing pope to Moses, who retreated to a mountain to pray. That same metaphor emerged a few days later, in Benedict's address at his next Sunday audience. "The Lord is calling me to climb the mountain, to dedicate myself more to prayer and contemplation," he said. Some analysts wondered whether Benedict was showing a spiritual kinship with Cardinal Ravasi.

During his last two weeks in office, the silent shadow of the departing Pope hovered over preparations for the conclave. He had appointed 67 of the cardinal-electors who would choose his successor—nearly the entire required two-thirds majority—and worked closely with most of the others during his years as prefect of the Congregation for the Doctrine of the Faith. Yet Benedict refused to become involved in the pre-conclave discussions. Moreover, his unusual exit encouraged cardinals themselves to do something unusual. As the American Vatican-watcher John L. Allen pointed out, there would be no papal funeral, tempting electors toward a sentimental obligation to honor the wishes of the deceased. The Pope's departure would not take place under ordinary circumstances, and neither would the election.

"Among you, the College of Cardinals, is also the future Pope, to whom I today promise my unconditioned reverence and obedience."

—*Benedict XVI during his farewell meeting with the College of Cardinals on February 28*

The general congregations

On Monday, March 4, the cardinals gathered for their first "general congregation." These gatherings prior to the conclave are open to all cardinals, and 143 prelates, including 103 electors, took part in the first Monday meeting. The top items on the agenda were planning for the papal election, weighing the needs of the universal Church, and discussing the requirements for the next pontiff. But a number of cardinals, especially those from outside Rome, pressed for consideration of other issues, especially the "Vatileaks" fiasco and the appearance of disorganization within the Roman Curia.

The Honduran Cardinal Oscar Rodriguez Maradiaga said that the cardinals hoped to learn more about the "Vatileaks" affair during the general congregations. The three cardinals who had undertaken an investigation of the affair, and reported confidentially to Pope Benedict, were all too old to participate in the conclave, but they would be present at the general congregations. They could not disclose the contents of their secret report without Benedict's permission, which he had not given. But Brazilian Cardinal Raymundo Damasceno Assis reasoned, "We certainly can ask for some information about the content of their report."

According to a report in the Italian daily *La Stampa*, Cardinals Christoph Schoenborn, Peter Erdö, and Walter Kasper

immediately demanded some information about the "Vatileaks" report. Another Italian daily, *La Repubblica*, reported that the chairman of the investigating panel, Cardinal Julian Herranz, told the congregation that their dossier did not contain any damaging information about any cardinal—a claim that, according to the newspaper report, prompted incredulous shaking of heads among the more skeptical electors.

While these reports were based on leaks, and could not be confirmed, Cardinal Schönborn proclaimed in a public statement that it was time to speak openly about the "mistakes and failures" of Vatican leadership. Cardinal Sean O'Malley of Boston, according to another leak from the general congregation, assigned much of the blame to the Vatican bureaucracy,

saying that the pontificate of Benedict XVI had not been "saved from the Curia."

Meanwhile other cardinals were looking beyond the immediate concerns about the gaffes of the Curia, and concentrating on the challenge of the New Evangelization. Colombian Cardinal Ruben Salazar Gomez observed that the universal Church is "much more, and much larger, than the internal workings of the Curia." The Czech Primate Dominik Duka said that "de-Christianization" of society and the collapse of the family were issues more important than Vatican leaks and infighting. Cardinal O'Malley reminded his colleagues that the pope should act not as an administrative disciplinarian but as a pastor: a shepherd rather than a sheriff, as he put it.

The Italian Cardinal Francesco Coccopalmiero reportedly suggested regular meetings of the Pope with the leaders of the Vatican congregations. His comment was welcomed by many others. The American Cardinal Daniel DiNardo told Vatican Radio that he had been surprised to realize that the Vatican offices worked separately, without the sort of coordination he expected from his own diocesan officials.

> "Certainly I don't know how long or when, but in the next 100 years there will certainly be a pope or popes from South America, possibly or less likely from an Asian country."
>
> *Cardinal George Pell of Sydney, Australia before the conclave*

As the general congregations continued each day, more than 100 cardinals had an opportunity to speak, and their interventions covered topics ranging from bioethics to Islam to the role of women in the Church. Many returned to the public perception of chaos in the Roman Curia. Cardinal Bertone, the *camerlengo*, provided a briefing on the situation facing the Vatican bank; several cardinals allegedly called for a wide debate on the future of that institution, which had drawn critical scrutiny from European banking regulators.

One cardinal's short address had a particularly strong impact on the general congregations. A few weeks after the papal election, Cardinal Jaime Ortega y Alamino of Havana—having secured the permission of the new Pope to share the information—disclosed that one prelate roused the attention of the assembly when he spoke about "going out into the streets to proclaim Jesus to everyone." Speaking in moderate tones but with a keen sense of urgency, the speaker said:

"Put simply, there are two images of the Church: a Church which evangelizes and comes out of herself, the *Dei Verbum religiose audiens et fidente proclamans*; and the worldly Church—living within herself, of herself, for herself. This should shed light on the possible changes and reforms which must be made for the salvation of souls."

That speaker, whose eloquent insights caused many other cardinals to snap to attention, was Cardinal Jorge Mario Bergoglio of Buenos Aires. From that moment forward, according to Cuban Cardinal Ortega, many cardinals began to see their Argentine colleague in a new light.

Final preparations

While they discussed who might become the next pope, the cardinals—and the thousands of journalists covering the events in Rome—also gave some thought to the question of who might be appointed to the powerful post of Secretary of State. Some officials with experience in the Roman Curia—allegedly including Cardinals Bertone and Giovanni Battista Re–were said to favor the election of a non-Italian cardinal, who would then appoint an Italian Secretary of State. Their favored candidate for the papacy, reporters said, was Cardinal Odilo Scherer of Sao Paulo.

Ironically, the proponents of a sweeping reform in the Roman Curia were said to favor an Italian, Cardinal Angelo Scola, because he had nothing to do with the administration of Vatican offices in recent years. So according to many reports swirling in the Italian press, the defenders of the Roman establishment were backing a foreign candidate for the papacy, while the "outsiders" were throwing their support behind an Italian. In a background conversation with a journalist, one cardinal said that he was "really scared" that the candidate supported by the Curia would enter the conclave with a few dozen votes, "and then they will pull it off before another candidate can be built up." Yet *La Repubblica* claimed that Cardinal Scola, the supposed candidate of the reformers, "has about 40 definite votes" before the conclave began. "Everything in the conclave will depend on the relationship between these two blocs"—the defenders of the Roman Curia and the advocates of reform—intoned *La Repubblica*.

On the way to the proceedings before the Conclave: Cardinal Bergoglio picks up the cardinal's red hat dropped by Canadian Cardinal Marc Ouellet.

Even as the speculation about conflicts among the cardinals intensified, the push for a speedy conclave eased. On March 5, the second day of the general congregations, the cardinals paused to send a telegram of greeting to Pope Emeritus Benedict in Castel Gandolfo (where a *paparazzo* photo showed him walking through the gardens of the papal residence), and decided to cancel two planned afternoon sessions. The cardinals were in no rush, it was clear.

On that same day, March 5, the Sistine Chapel was closed to visitors. Vatican workmen would need time to prepare the site for the cardinals' meeting: installing a wooden floor over the unevenly worn marble, setting up tables and chairs, and installing electronic jamming devices to guard against any possible eavesdropping or communication with the outside world. (The workers even temporarily removed climate-control monitors inside the Sistine Chapel, since they might be mistaken for cameras or microphones.) This would be the 25th conclave held in the Sistine Chapel, although it was only in 1996 that Pope John Paul II officially designated it as the site of papal elections.

During the general congregations, some cardinals were upset with the steady criticism of the Roman Curia and the accompanying media uproar. Cardinal Bertone was evidently annoyed when the remarks of Cardinal Joao Braz de Aviz,

the Brazilian prefect of the Congregation for Religious, were leaked to the press. The Secretary of State defended himself before his colleagues, earning spontaneous applause, and many cardinals agreed that the insatiable media appetite for stories—nearly all of them unconfirmed—complicated their work.

The tendency among reporters to see the conclave as a struggle for power also irritated Church leaders. Bishop Juan Ignacio Arrieta, the secretary of the Pontifical Council for Legislative Texts, reminded a Vatican Radio audience that the conclave would be "primarily a prayerful event." He added: "It follows a liturgical text specially created for the papal election, the *Ordo Rituum Conclavis*. Cardinals who had participated in previous conclaves supported his remarks, recalling the many rosaries they had said while waiting through the lengthy process of casting and counting ballots. "This may seem a bit odd," said Vienna's Cardinal Schönborn, "but it's not by chance that we meet in a chapel. The papal election is a matter of prayer, to find out who is chosen by God." Even before the conclave the cardinals announced that they felt the desire to pray together, and scheduled a special evening service in St. Peter's Basilica for that purpose.

The reporters covering the papal transition—numbering over 5,000 accredited by the Vatican press office, from

Crowds in St. Peter's Square watching video screens, waiting for news from the conclave.

more than 60 different countries—were less interested in prayer than in speculation about the politics of the conclave, or colorful "human-interest" stories about the latest developments at the Vatican. There were thousands of reports about a German man who dressed up as a bishop and succeeded in mingling with the cardinals for a few minutes before he was escorted out by the Swiss Guards. Father Lombardi, the Vatican press spokesman, declined to comment on the odd incident except to say that, when it came to the conclave: "All the cardinals are genuine."

By Thursday, March 7, all the cardinal-electors had arrived in Rome. Under the terms of the rule recently amended by Pope Benedict, the cardinals could now set a date for the conclave, and they did: Tuesday, March 12. Father Lombardi pointed out that the much-discussed conflict over the date had failed to materialize. The Vatican spokesman told reporters that he expected a relatively short conclave.

On the Sunday before the election, as the cardinals fanned out across Rome to celebrate Mass in the titular churches that had been assigned to them when they received their red hats, a group of journalists visited the Sistine Chapel to see the preparations for the conclave. Just to the left of the front door stood two gray stoves, each about three feet high. The stove on the right was used to burn the cardinals' ballots after each round of voting. It was etched with the dates of the papal elections from 1939 through 2005, although the markings were difficult to read. The stove on the left was reserved for the chemical dyes that would change the appearance of the smoke, signaling to the outside world when a pope had been elected. The shiny copper chimneys of the two stoves were joined and ran up the Chapel wall to the roof.

Below Michelangelo's "Last Judgment" on the front wall, the workers had arranged two rows of tables and chairs along the side walls, making the Sistine Chapel look vaguely like a banquet hall. The 115 cardinal-electors would be sitting at these tables, crowded close together. At each place was a name tag, a small red leather folder embossed with the gold symbol of the *sede vacante* period, a pen, a Bible, and the *Ordo Rituum Conclavis.*

Exit Omnes!

On Tuesday morning, March 12, the cardinal-electors moved into rooms at the Domus Sanctae Marthae, the Vatican residence where they would stay, isolated from the world, until a new pontiff was chosen. Their rooms were modest dormitory-style units, assigned by lottery. (The most attractive accommodations in the building, a modest suite of rooms, was left empty, to be used by the new Pope after his election, until renovations could be completed in the papal apartments on the third floor of the apostolic palace.) From this residence the cardinals could walk or take shuttle buses across the Vatican to the Sistine Chapel. Their route would be guarded by Vatican gendarmes. Their bus drivers, and the handful of people assigned to cook and clean at the Domus Sanctae Marthae, were sworn to silence about the cardinals' discussions.

Before the conclave began, the cardinals joined in celebrating a special Mass for the occasion, the *Missa pro Eligendo Pontifice*, with the dean of the College of Cardinals, Cardinal Angelo Sodano, presiding. In his homily the Italian cardinal spoke of the "shining pontificate" of Benedict XVI, drawing a minute of applause, and urged prayers for a "Pope with a generous heart." The Mass was broadcast on giant screens in St. Peter's Square. As the ceremony ended, a sweeping downpour emptied the piazza.

On that same Tuesday morning, *Corriere della Sera*, the newspaper in Milan, claimed that Cardinal Scola, the head of that archdiocese, "already has 50 votes" entering the conclave. Cardinal Scherer, the Brazilian, supposedly had 15 to 18. New York's Cardinal Timothy Dolan was said to have 10 to 15 votes, with another 10 to 15 likely to go to the Canadian, Cardinal Marc Ouellet. The name "Bergoglio" did not figure at all in the newspaper's predictions.

In the afternoon the 115 electors made their solemn procession into the Sistine

Chapel, chanting the Litany of the Saints and the *Veni Creator Spiritus* along the way. They bowed before the altar, and one by one they solemnly swore to keep the secrets of the conclave, to protect the freedom of the Church, and to take no part in any conspiracy. The Vatican television center showed the line of red-robed cardinals taking their places, some of them raising their heads to look at Michelangelo's ceiling frescoes, portraying scenes from the Book of Genesis. Cardinal Giovanni Battista Re, acting as dean of the College of Cardinals (since Cardinal Sodano was too old to enter the conclave) led the proceedings, administering the oaths.

When all the oaths had been taken, the Vatican's master of ceremonies, Msgr. Guido Marini, issued the order: "*Exit omnes!*" ("Everyone out!")

With that, all the aides, acolytes, technicians, and cameramen who had entered the Sistine Chapel with the cardinals filed out. At 5:43 pm, Msgr. Marini closed the doors of the Sistine Chapel. Now the electors were alone and—save for the smoke that would issue from the chimneys—the public had no way to know what was happening inside the conclave.

The public did know, at least, that there would be just one vote scheduled that evening before the cardinals retired for the night. At 7:41 p.m. the first smoke arose from the roof of the Sistine Chapel. It was pitch black. The *sede vacante* period would last at least one more day.

A Church that is not
closed in on itself: an
open-air Mass in 1998.

The Bishop from the Ends of the Earth

He loves the tango; he was trained as a chemist; in his youth he had a regular girlfriend, and planned to marry her. For a Pope, Francis has an unusual life story. His ancestors are from Italy, but he has rarely traveled outside his own native Argentina. His life has not been punctuated by great public successes. He never calls attention to himself, preferring to stay in the background. He was pulled out of obscurity to be made a bishop, and was preparing for a quiet retirement when he was elected Pope.

Jorge Mario Bergoglio is no ordinary man. As a bishop he proved himself a friend of the poor, often visiting the slums on the outskirts of Buenos Aires. As a public figure he has played a delicate and sometimes controversial role, first during the years when his country lived under a military dictatorship, then again when a new government pushed to legalize abortion and same-sex marriage. He has regularly provoked strong reactions, good or bad, from those who work with him and those touched by his work. Yet he has clearly never been impressed with himself. On his gravestone he wanted a simple inscription: "Jorge Bergoglio, priest."

"Rent a garage, if you can."

The new Pope "will surprise us all," predicted Cardinal Joachim Meisner of Cologne on the night after the conclave's conclusion; but "he will have to divulge a lot about his life, which is probably the down side." The German cardinal was alluding to the pontiff's reluctance to discuss his private life. But another aspect of the "disadvantage" soon became apparent: Hardly anyone really knew Jorge Mario Bergoglio.

In the first hours after the papal election, reporters began probing into the new Pope's background, searching for information or anecdotes that would help a curious world understand this 265th successor to St. Peter. What they unearthed formed a portrait of a sober Jesuit who, as Archbishop of Buenos Aires, refused the use of an official car, preferring to ride the city's buses. (Many residents of Buenos Aires had seen their archbishop rushing through the streets in his simple black clerical garb; no one, it seems, could remember spotting him at a fashionable reception or cocktail party.) He was once a heavy smoker, but kicked the habit. He still loves the tango, explaining that "it comes from deep inside me." He enjoys the writing of Jorge Louis Borges and the music of Beethoven; his favorite film is a Danish work, *Babette's Feast*.

Above all the portrait was of a simple man. Pope Francis did not begin chanting the gospel of poverty and humility when he appeared on the central loggia of St. Peter's; he had been practicing those virtues for years, mostly unnoticed, at the "ends of the earth." He rejected the luxury of the palatial archbishop's residence and took a small apartment. He did his own shopping, cooked his own meals, made his own bed, washed his own dirty socks. This unusual man, whom so few people knew, turned out to be a simple yet deeply religious man, who wanted to bring the mercy of God to the people. In his spare time he visited the slums on the edges of the city. "I do not say that man is good or bad, I simply believe in him, in his dignity and greatness," he said.

"Interviews are not my forté," then-Cardinal Bergoglio once remarked, and for that reason he seldom sat down to speak on the record with reporters. When two journalists sought a formal interview, he advised them to publish excerpts from his sermons and essays instead. When he did finally

agree to a series of interviews—which would become the book *El Jesuita*, with a foreword by his friend Rabbi Abraham Skorka—he ended each session by asking the journalists dubiously: "Do you really think that this will be useful to anyone?"

"We have to get out of ourselves," the future Pope said in one of his rare interviews, in 2012, with the Italian journalist Andrea Tornielli of the daily *La Stampa*. He drew a distinction between the relatively comfortable life of a parish and the difficulties facing people in the outside world. The Church, he said, must face that outside world and "head for the periphery," bringing Christ to the people on the margins. "We need to avoid the spiritual sickness of a Church that is self-centered," he added, sounding one of the common themes of his reflections on the life of the Church; "when a Church becomes like that, it grows sick." There are dangers associated with this approach, he conceded:

"It is true that going out onto the street, as with every man and every woman, implies the risk of accidents happening. But if the Church remains closed in, self-centered, it will grow old. And if I had to choose between a bumpy Church that goes out onto the streets and a sick self-centered Church, I would definitely choose the former."

In Buenos Aires the archbishop encouraged his priests always to "make contact with the families who do not come to us." The Church, he explained, needs to reach out to "those who have drifted away" and those who are indifferent. How can this be accomplished? "We organize missions in public squares, where many people usually gather: we pray, we celebrate the Eucharist, we offer baptism which we administer after a brief preparation . . . . We also try to reach out to people who are far away, via digital means, the Web and text messaging."

In another interview the Argentine archbishop laid down the general principle that "anything that can lead to the path to God is good." He said that he instructed his priests to do their regular pastoral duties and then "leave the door open" to other possibilities. Sociologists of religion, he said, had estimated that the influence of a parish in Buenos Aires extended to a radius of about .33 of a mile, but parishes are separated by distances averaging about 1.2 miles. So how could pastors reach the people outside the limits of their own parishes? "If you can, rent a garage," said the archbishop, "and if you can find one or two laymen available, don't hold them back!" The laymen could care for the people, provide a bit of religious instruction, and even bring Communion, he said. Cardinal Bergoglio recalled: "A pastor then said to me, 'But Father,

if we do that, then won't people stop coming to church?'

'Well,' I replied, 'Are they coming to Mass now?'

'No,' he admitted."

Priests depend on lay people for help out of necessity, the archbishop said, in order to open out their horizons. But the danger, he continued,

Wedding picture (December 12, 1935) of the Pope's parents, Regina Maria Sivori and Mario Giuseppe Bergoglio.

is that they might give lay people a clerical mentality. "The priests make clerics out of the laity, and then the laity ask us to make clerics of them," he said, decrying this as "a sinful complicity."

Cardinal Bergoglio pointed to the example of Japan, where Christian communities did not see a priest for more than 200 years. Yet when missionaries did finally return to Japan they found that the faithful had been baptized, married in church services, and given a Christian burial when they died. Lay Catholics had preserved the faith intact, even without priests.

Every Catholic can be active in promoting the faith, the Argentine prelate

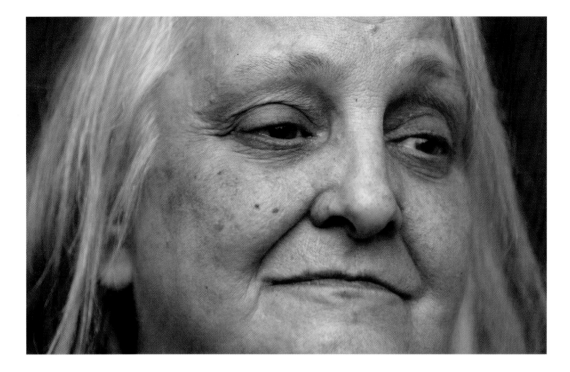

Maria Elena Bergoglio on the day of her brother's election to Pope.

insisted. Even if Catholics are divorced and remarried—and therefore ineligible to receive Communion—there is no reason why they cannot help out in their parishes. The cardinal remarked in *El Jesuita* that there is always "plenty to do."

Hard-headed people from Piedmont

Jorge Mario Bergoglio was born on December 17, 1936 in Buenos Aires to a family of immigrants from Italy. His father, Mario Giuseppe (whose third name, incidentally, was Francesco), hailed from the Asti province in northern Italy's Piedmont region. Along with other members of his family he traveled to Argentina on the ship *Giulio Cesare* in January 1929. Many Italians made the same trip to escape poverty. For the Bergoglio family, the motives for immigration may have been more complicated. "The

family wasn't doing well economically, but we weren't starving, either," said Maria Elena Bergoglio, the sister of the future Pope. At the time the shadow of Mussolini's fascist government was falling across Italy. Maria Elena recalled: "I heard my father say again and again that it was the fascist coup that really caused him to leave the country."

In the little village of Portacomaro Stazione, north of Asti, the old Italian house once inhabited by the Bergoglio family is still standing. In 2001, when he traveled to Italy to receive a cardinal's red hat from Pope John Paul II, the archbishop stopped by Portacomaro Stazione for a day, accompanied by his sister, and is reported to have taken a sample of Piedmontese

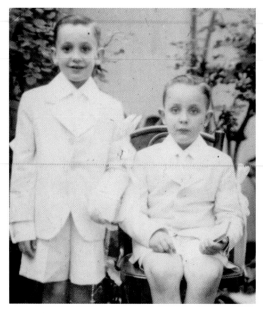

Brothers Jorge and Oscar Bergoglio.

Jorge Bergoglio's father Mario Giuseppe (center) with his parents Giovanni Bergoglio and Margarita Vasallo, Pope Francis' grandparents.

soil with him as a keepsake. "It was really moving," said Maria Elena. "The area is gorgeous, and we walked together through the hills. And then to see the house where my father was born, the garden where he played as a child, the basement where our uncle made wine—incredible!"

Although he thinks of himself primarily as an Argentinian, Pope Francis held an Italian passport as well as his Argentine one, and in his youth he spoke Italian with his girlfriend. "That was our way of being co-conspirators," remembered the one-time girlfriend years later, after "Jorge" had been elected to the papacy. Like many children of immigrant families, Jorge sometimes felt two hearts beating in his chest. Once, with tears in his eyes, he recited from memory *"Rassa Nostrana"* ("Our Race"), a poem by

Nina Costa, for friends. The poem speaks of the people of Piedmont as *drit e sincer* ("straightforward and honest"), *teste quadre* ("hard-headed people"). Costa writes: "They do not talk much, but they know what they are saying. Even if they go slow, they go far."

In a sense the man who is now Bishop of Rome seems to have felt a yearning for Italy, the land of his forefathers, all his life. "According to its Greek roots, 'nostalgia' means a desire to return to a place," he mused in *El Jesuita*. The *Odyssey* speaks of longing as well. It is a dimension of being human." Oddly, though, the younger Bergoglio probably did not inherit this longing from his father, who, having left his homeland when he was just over 20 years old, never turned back, and spoke only Spanish with his five children. For him, any lingering

Pope Francis as a teenager, taken from his sister Maria Elena's album.

Two kinds of apparel: one for mass, one for his favorite soccer club San Lorenzo de Almagro.

emotions about Italy had become "something that he had to bottle up, something he had left behind," Cardinal Bergoglio said.

The father found work first in Parana, as a bookkeeper in a road-construction firm that three of his brothers had set up after emigrating seven years earlier. Then he moved his family to the middle-class Flores neighborhood of Buenos Aires, where he worked as a corporate accountant. He was determined that his children would grow up as Argentines, and he spoke to them in fluent Spanish. Still Maria Elena Bergoglio remembers:

"But at night, when he met with our uncles, they all fell into Italian or into the Piedmontese dialect. Then they would speak of the beauty of their home, which

remained like a dream for them their whole lives, and of World War I, in which they had fought. And they complained about fascism."

Young Jorge's grandmother Rosa regularly picked him up in the morning, and to help out his mother she brought him to her own home to spend the day, then brought him back in the evening. His grandparents spoke to each other in the Piedmontese dialect, and during those days the boys learned the language. More importantly, his grandmother taught him his prayers, and told him stories of the saints, giving him a foundation in faith that would equip him for life.

"If we don't get married, then I will become a priest"

Young Jorge collected stamps, and like all the children in the Flores district he

His up-to-date member's pass to San Lorenzo de Almagro sports club.

The Bergoglio family was not poor, but was certainly far from affluent. There was no family car and no summer vacation trips, but the future Pope says "we wanted for nothing." The children were expected to contribute to the family's welfare, beginning at an early age. When the children came home from school they would often find their mother—who was left severely disabled after the birth of her fifth child—peeling potatoes. Regina Maria would tell the children how to cook their dinner, and they would carry out her instructions. (The future Pope learned to enjoy cooking; he would later cook for college students, and continued making his own meals regularly until his election as Roman pontiff.) At his father's prompting he went to work at age 13 for a cleaning service. After a few years he moved up to administrative tasks. Still later he applied the knowledge he was gaining in his study of chemistry to work in a clinical laboratory. Jorge would work from 7 in the morning until 1 in the afternoon; then after an hour for lunch he would go to school until 8.

played soccer. He joined the San Lorenzo athletic club, which plays in a stadium in his old neighborhood; he remains an active member. "He was a normal teenager, well behaved and a good student," reports his sister Maria Elena. "He has always protected me, because I was the youngest." He played cards with his father, and they shared an interest in sports. (The father played basketball with the San Lorenzo team, and sometimes Jorge would accompany him.) With his mother, Regina Maria, he listened to music. "Every Saturday afternoon at 2 o'clock we listened to the operas, which were broadcast on state radio," said Cardinal Bergoglio. Before the broadcast his mother would explain the opera to the children and call their attention to the most memorable arias. When the children grew restless she would find ways to keep them interested. "During *Otello* she said, 'Look out, he's going to kill them now!'" the future Pope remembers.

"I thank my father for sending me to work," Cardinal Bergoglio said. "Work was one of the things that taught me the most." He remembers particularly the laboratory, where his boss was a woman with militant leftist political sympathies: a woman who was later put to death by Argentina's military government. While working for her, Jorge Bergoglio read the Communist circular *Propositos* with interest. "It helped me in my political education," he reports. "But I've never been a Communist."

St. Ignatius and the Jesuits

In 1534, 17 years after Martin Luther sparked the Reformation, St. Ignatius, a former professional soldier from Loyola in Spain, founded the Society of Jesus with a handful of friends. Inspired by the founder's Spiritual Exercises, which remain the core of Jesuit spirituality, the Jesuits quickly became the vanguard of the Catholic revival known as the Counter-Reformation. They founded schools and oversaw the building of Baroque churches, advised princes, and made themselves available to the Pope as a sort of spiritual rapid-deployment force. In addition to the usual religious vows of poverty, chastity, and obedience, the Jesuits took another vow to be readily available to fulfill any assignment for the Pope.

From their first days the Jesuits have encountered controversy. Their military-style organizational structure and tight discipline, along with the fact that they wore no distinctive religious habit, encouraged rumors of conspiracy. Because of their sworn loyalty they were seen in some societies as a subversive element, while in others their close relations with kings and princes made commoners associate them with the ruling elite. In 1773, Pope Clement XIV suppressed the Jesuit order because of complaints of political intriguing. (The Society was reinstated by Pope Pius VII in 1814.) Similar accusations have dogged the order to this day. As a Jesuit provincial in Argentina, the future Pope Francis wrestled with the problems that arose when many Jesuits joined in movements for radical political change in Latin America.

Jesuit missionaries, led by St. Francis Xavier, became pioneers in several respects. Jesuits attained high positions in the court of the Chinese emperor; evangelized the Indian tribes of North America; and for a short time established an idealistic regime in Paraguay, which became the subject for the award-winning film *The Mission*. The Jesuit order remains strongly associated with higher education, administering hundreds of colleges and universities around the world including the Gregorian University in Rome, Université Saint Joseph in Beirut, Catholic University in San Salvador, and Georgetown, Fordham, Marquette, and the Loyola universities in the United States. Prominent Jesuit theologians of the 20th century included Karl Rahner, Teilhard de Chardin, and the American Cardinal Avery Dulles. There are nearly 18,000 members of the Society of Jesus in the world today.

Ignatius of Loyola, founder of the Jesuit Order. Portrait from the 17th century, artist unknown.

The Catholic Church in Argentina

Half of the Catholics worldwide live in Latin America. Since the days of Columbus, the Spanish conquest of the continent and missionaries proclaiming the Gospel have gone hand in hand. The diversity of the Church is demonstrated by the many martyrs who served the needy, Christian resistance to oppression, the dedication to the poor, an intense reverence for the Virgin Mary, as well as many traditions of popular beliefs that often meld with pre-Christian practices.

In Argentina, the second largest country in South America, 93% of the population is Catholic. Surveys regularly confirm that the church is the most trusted institution in the country. According to the German Latin American relief organization Adveniat, this is due to the Argentine Church "literally taking on the role of a political opposition, being the spokesperson for the poor and outcast, doing their best to authentically embody the option for the poor." Nonetheless the Bishops Conference is known to be divided between "an ecclesiastically moderate and a socially progressive leaning" to which Jorge Mario Bergoglio belongs, and "a deeply conservative and traditionalistic tendency."

The relationship between Church and State has been uneven in recent decades. On occasion, the Church supported the State politically, while on other occasions "there was rivalry between them", said Joseph Oerhlein, of the *Frankfurter Allgemeine Zeitung*. During the "leaden times" of the military dictatorship (1976–1983), the church also played an ambiguous role. Some Catholic clerics worked together with the torturers, others came to the defense of victims. Under the aegis of Bergoglio in 2000, Argentine bishops formulated an admission of guilt for the many church people who were involved in crimes against the people during the junta. State-Church relationships have deteriorated under the presidency of the two Kirchners (first Nestor and then, after his death, his wife Cristina). Bergoglio accused the ruling elite of corruption and indifference to the poor—to the point of manipulating official statistics on the percentage of poor in Argentina: 9% according to the government, 30% according to international assessments.

Jorge Bergoglio's childhood sweetheart, Amalia Damonte. Now they are both 76.

Buenos Aires, Argentina: Front view of Herminia Brumana Square where Pope played football as a child.

Pope Francis' parental home in Flores, Buenos Aires.

The laboratory boss was not the only woman in his life, however. There was also Amalia, a girl who lived in the same neighborhood. She was the same age as Jorge, and her family too had immigrated from Piedmont. Their friendship began when they were only two years old, and steadily grew. Although they did not attend the same school—boys and girls were separated—they began spending their afternoons together, playing on the sidewalks or in the neighborhood parks. As they grew a bit older, Jorge began talking about how they might spend their lives together, and by the time they were 12 he wrote her letters describing the house in which they would live after they were married. At that point Amalia's father intervened. Believing that the children were too young to be thinking so seriously about marriage, he forbade Jorge from courting his daughter, and he obeyed that order.

Looking back on the youthful romance after her old friend was elected Pope, Amalia Damonte said that it was "a very innocent thing." Their parents need not have worried, she says. At the same time, she told reporters, in those days it was unthinkable that children would defy their parents' wishes. Yet Amalia believes there might have been another reason why their romance did not flourish. Even at that time, she says, Jorge was considering the priesthood. "He once told me: If we don't get married, then I will become a priest!"

So Jorge and Amalia went their separate ways. She became a bookkeeper, married, and when her husband died eventually married again. She now has three children and six grandchildren. After years she moved back into their old neighborhood, and now lives in the house next to what was once the Bergoglio home. She had not seen her old boyfriend in 60 years. "But when I learned of his election as Pope," she says, "it was an immense pleasure for me. I said aloud: May God bless you!"

In *El Jesuita*, Cardinal Bergoglio does not hesitate to mention that he had a girlfriend in his youth, but neither does he dwell on the memory. She was part of "the group of friends with whom I went out to dance," he said. The cardinal said that he only felt the vocational call to the priesthood later.

A confession that changed everything

Along with hard work and youthful romance, Jorge Mario Bergoglio was also introduced to serious illness at an early age. As a young man he nearly died of pneumonia. He recalled having a high fever, anxiously asking his mother what was happening to him, and receiving no reply, because the doctors had no clear answers. His right lung was surgically removed, and he endured several months of painful recuperation. During that recovery period, he grew tired of visitors who told him that he would soon be better. But he has fond memories of Sister Dolores, the nun who had prepared him for his First

Communion. When she visited she told him: "You are suffering like Jesus." That thought had a powerful impact on the young Jorge. Suffering is not a virtue, he reflected in *El Jesuita*. "But the way we encounter suffering can be virtuous."

At around the same time, the thought that he might be called to the priesthood began to play on Jorge's mind daily. However Pope Francis points to a single decisive experience—a "Damascus experience"—that settled the matter in his mind. It was on September 27, 1953, when he was 17 years old. He was preparing for a school celebration, and his classmates were waiting for him at the train station. Jorge stopped for a quick visit in the church of San José de Flores, a few blocks from his parents' house. There he saw a priest he did not recognize, standing near the last confessional to the left of the altar, and decided on the spur of the moment that he would ask that priest to hear his confession. That confession would change his life. Jorge experienced a powerful sense of encounter, and felt an unmistakable call. "I realized that someone was waiting for me," he said.

Those friends at the train station were waiting in vain; Jorge never came back. He had decided to become a priest. "This is the experience of religion: the wonder, the meeting with someone who's waiting for you," Cardinal Bergoglio wrote. "You look for Him, but He has already been looking for you." He learned later that the young priest who had heard his confession on that fateful day died of leukemia a year afterward.

During his Jesuit schooling, Jorge Bergoglio taught literature and psychology at the Colegio del Salvador in Buenos Aires. (1966)

His father took Jorge's decision well, but not his mother. She encouraged him to finish his studies, to work for a while, to wait. Four years later, with his degree in chemical engineering in hand, he entered the Jesuit novitiate. The date was March 11, 1956: exactly 57 years before the opening of the conclave that would elect him as Roman pontiff. His mother refused to visit him in the seminary. They had not really quarreled, he says, but "everything was going too fast for her."

Jorge had made a clear decision to become a priest, but he was less certain at first about entering a religious order. He gravitated toward the Jesuits, he said, because "the Society of Jesus used a military language, because a climate of obedience and discipline prevailed." The missionary mandate of the Jesuits also fascinated him. He thought of going to Japan as a missionary, following in the footsteps of the great Jesuit missionary, St. Francis Xavier. But his health did not allow for that possibility.

"Jorge Bergoglio, priest"

Having become a Jesuit, Jorge Bergoglio went through the extensive training typical of the order: studying the humanities in Chile, then heading back to Buenos Aires for courses in philosophy at the College of San Jose San Miguel. In 1964 and 1965 he taught literature and psychology in Santa Fe. Then he returned to the capital for more work in theology, finally graduating from San Miguel in 1970.

Maria Elena Bergoglio remembers the Jorge Mario of those student years as a practical joker, much like his father. The Cardinal—the only other survivor among the five Bergoglio children—does not disagree. Even while wearing his clerical collar, he taught his godson Jorge the most colorful insults. Once when the little child shouted out one of those epithets during the middle of Mass, Jorge shook with laughter after the ceremony. In another incident, Jorge Mario dipped his godson's pacifier in whiskey.

On December 13, 1969, just a few days before his 33rd birthday, Jorge Bergoglio was ordained to the priesthood. For him this was the essential point of all his work. One year later, in Alcala de Henares, he took his final vows as a Jesuit. A series of assignments followed: novice master in San Miguel, professor of theology, rector of colleges and faculties, and—most precious to the young priest—his first experience as a pastor.

In 1973 Bergoglio was elected Provincial for the Jesuits in Argentina; he would hold that post for six years. Each young Argentine man who wanted to become a Jesuit was required to petition Father Bergoglio, and so he met Guillermo Ortiz, who is now a Jesuit priest and director of Spanish-language programming for Vatican Radio. Looking back on his first impressions of the new Pope, Father Ortiz said that Father Bergoglio, who was then a theology professor, was an exacting instructor. "He demanded a lot, but he didn't leave us to fend for ourselves," he said. Later, in the 1980s, Ortiz was a parish priest in a working-class neighborhood. Again he came under the influence of Father Bergoglio:

"We learned a lot, because he sent us out on the road. We were to visit the sick, give catechism classes to children. We went out every Saturday and Sunday to be with the people: the workers, those carrying heavy burdens. It was an extraordinary experience."

The secret of his old mentor's life was, and is, prayer, Father Ortiz believes. Father

The Argentine Dictatorship

Throughout history, Argentina has had several dictators, but the dictatorship between 1976 and 1983 was unparalleled in its viciousness. Like the regime of General Pinochet in Chile three years previous, the coup plotters of Buenos Aires in 1976 "actually strove to bring the entire country under its subjugation", Rainer Huhle of the Nurnberg Human Rights Center explained in an interview with Radio Vatican. They wanted absolute control of "every single aspect of civilian life"—a totalitarian aspiration. "There had been bloody and autocratic regimes in the past, but the greater part of the population was untouched by them."

The United States kept quiet. The world was still in the clutches of the Cold War and the Argentine military purported to be allies in the struggle against Communism, while they murdered tens of thousands of oppositionists and engineered the "disappearance" (*desaparecidos*) of many people. At the time the Catholic Church, not only in Argentina, but in all of Latin America, was "deeply divided". "There was a strong undercurrent of 'Liberation Theology' . . . and then there was the traditional church which over the centuries had accomodated various regimes."

While the Catholic Church in Chile, after short hesitation, sided with the victims, it was the other way around in Argentina. "The priests and bishops who were against the dictatorship were a tiny minority, and accordingly persecuted. The main part of the institutional church more or less adapted well to the regime." Two bishops who had spoken out against the generals died in staged car accidents. The police chaplain, Christian von Wernich, participated in 42 kidnappings, 31 counts of torture and 7 murders—for which he was sentenced to life imprisonment in 2007.

Countless parents grieve for their children, the *desaparecidos*—victims of disappearance, arbitrary arrest and torture—under the Argentine military dictatorship 1976–1983.

Bergoglio went to bed early in those days, but was already up at 4 in the morning to pray. His words and deeds clearly grew from his conversations with God. In Argentina, Father Ortiz says, everyone knows about Cardinal Bergoglio's sermons against exploitation and corruption. "But when you listen to him, he doesn't speak as if he is speaking from some university chair; he speaks to you directly," he says. "When he talks about drug addiction, then you realize that he is talking about a person he has really listened to." Father Ortiz often saw Cardinal Bergoglio take to the streets of Buenos Aires, on his way to visit someone who was sick, or speak with a pastor. During the days Cardinal Bergoglio worked as an archbishop, but in the evenings he was just an ordinary pastor.

"He has a holistic view of things," says Father Ortiz. "He learns from what he sees; he puts things together. His ability to think in large terms, so to speak, has always impressed me. He is a great leader."

Nevertheless Father Ortiz never expected to see his old provincial as Pope. "I knew that he was important to the conclave, because of his experience, his presence, his personal history," he says. "But I did not expect it." When the new Pope's name was announced, "I was speechless. I had to make the live broadcast on the radio and found absolutely no words."

A Mass for the dictator

The Buenos Aires in which Father Bergoglio became the Jesuit provincial, seen in the black-and-white photos of the day, resembles Paris. Families stroll the wide boulevards of the city; the men wear hats and neckties and serious expressions. But that picture was soon to change. A series of economic and political crises shook Argentina in the 1970s. Then in March 1976, military leaders led by Jorge Videla, then the commander-in-chief of the armed forces, overthrew President Isabel Peron—the widow of the colorful demagogue Juan Peron, who had died two years earlier—and dissolved the country's parliament. Seven years of military dictatorship followed, accompanied by the opposition of left-wing guerillas.

Many of Argentina's bishops sympathized with the military regime. They believed the generals' assurances that the nation's government would be guided by Christian principles, and emergency measures were needed to ward off the threat of anarchy. At first an economic recovery seemed to vindicate the generals' leadership. Most of the bishops chose to remain silent about human-rights violations that became more and more blatant. At just one notorious detention center, on the grounds of the ESMA (Escuela de Mecanica de la Armada) naval academy in Buenos Aires, thousands of people were tortured to death.

Where did Father Bergoglio stand during those unhappy times? In the days following his election to the papacy, many media outlets asked that question, and tracked the Argentine prelate's actions during those years carefully, looking for clues about his relationship with the generals. The Ameri-

Undated portrait of the Bergoglio family. Jorge Mario can be recognized by his cassock.

can filmmaker Michael Moore even thought he had found a photo in which Bergoglio administered Communion to the dictator Jorge Videla himself; it turned out, however, that the priest in the photo was not Bergoglio.

It could have been, though. The Jesuit provincial had indeed once celebrated Mass for the Videla family, as he admitted in a 2010 interview. At the time he was looking for an opportunity to speak with Videla, to intercede for some of his priests, who had been imprisoned by the regime. Toward that end he insinuated himself into the dictator's house, arranging for the priest who was scheduled to say Mass to call in sick. After Mass he approached Videla to make his plea for the release of the detained Jesuits.

That the Jesuit provincial had direct relations with the dictator—and also worked to build up a relationship with Admiral Emilio Massera, regarded as a particularly brutal member of the military regime—caught up with him a few decades later. After Argentina's transition to democracy, when reporters began to research that dark era, there were suspicions that Bergoglio—who by now was Archbishop of Buenos Aires—had made his own peace with the regime.

Tale of Two Jesuits

Within hours after the election of Pope Francis was announced, newspapers around the world began carrying stories about a particularly controversial case in which the future pontiff—then Argentina's Jesuit provincial—was accused of denouncing two Jesuit priests who were detained for months by the military regime.

The whole affair is complicated by the fact that at the time when the two priests were kidnapped, they had already been at odds with their Jesuit order, and thus with their provincial. Fathers Orlando Yorio and Franz Jalics had been involved with the active resistance against the military rule. Father Bergoglio warned them against such partisan political activity, but they persisted. As he grew more worried about their situation, he invited them to come live with him in the provincial's residence, so that they might be safe. Again they ignored him, consciously risking arrest by continuing their public activism.

Moreover, Cardinal Bergoglio revealed later, Father Yorio and Jalics had sought to set up their own community, and had drawn up plans for a new residence in a Buenos Aires slum. When the provincial told them that they would have to choose between those plans and their commitment to the Society of Jesus, the two asked to be released from their Jesuit vows, he said. Yorio's request had been tentatively accepted shortly before the military coup. But as an ex-Jesuit he would not enjoy the order's protection from the regime, and Jalics, as a Jesuit on his way out, would not be much safer.

Beginning in 1974, the two priests had been living and working in the slums, and had the formal approval of their Jesuit superior despite his obvious misgivings. Although their opposition to the military regime was overt, they adamantly insisted that they had no contacts with the guerillas engaged in violent resistance against the government. However, one layman who had been working with them left their little community and joined the guerillas. Nine months later, when he was captured and interrogated by the military, he said—falsely, it seems—that he had kept in touch with the two Jesuits.

In 1976, on that testimony, Jalics and Yorio were arrested. After questioning them for five days, Jalics says, the officer in charge of their interrogation said: "Fathers, you were not to blame. I will make sure that you return to the slum." Despite that assurance, however, they were not released. They remained in custody, often blindfolded and chained, for five months.

When the two were finally released, they left Argentina immediately. Having been in prison, unable to communicate with the outside world, they had no idea why they had been detained so long. But Yorio harbored a suspicion that his provincial had been involved, and told the world that he thought Father Bergoglio had denounced them. Father Matthew Lamb, a theologian who became acquainted with some of the priests who had been working in the slums, points out that Yorio made that charge "before he was able to learn about what in fact his provincial had done."

After the fall of the military regime, when he was questioned about the two priests, then-Cardinal Bergoglio testified that he had "campaigned like crazy for them" during their months in prison. He wrote to a brother of Father Jalics, saying "I have made many approaches to the government for your brother's release. I consider this matter to be my affair. The difficulties that your brother and I have had over religious life have nothing to do with it."

Franz Jalics.

Orlando Yorio is now dead. But after Cardinal Bergoglio was elected to the papacy, Franz Jalics, who is now living in Germany, said that he wished the new pope well. Long after their release, he disclosed, he and Yorio "had the opportunity to discuss the events with Father Bergoglio." After that discussion, he said, the three had concelebrated Mass "and embraced solemnly." "The fact is: Orlando Yorio and I were not denounced by Father Bergoglio," said Jalics.

Maria Elena Bergoglio, the Pope's youngest sister, with her son Jorge, Francis' godson. (March 17, 2013)

Jorge Bergoglio (l) Provincial Superior of Argentine Jesuits, celebrating Mass with Superior General Pedro Arrupe (r).

The archbishop disagreed. Defending himself in interviews and court hearings, he explained what he had done and why he had done it.

Jorge Bergoglio, 1973.

Maria Elena Bergoglio is outraged by the suggestion that her brother would have supported a dictatorial government. "Do you really think this possible?" she asks. "That would mean that he had forgotten the lesson that our father taught us, with his own tough decision"—a reference to their father's choice to leave Italy, escaping a fascist regime. "Of course there were dark times, and you had to be careful," she allows. "But it has been proven that he helped many victims."

Rabbi Abraham Skorka, Cardinal Bergoglio's friend in Buenos Aires, says much the same thing:

"It is not true that he collaborated with the military, and I say this as a representative of a community that was severely affected by the generals. On the contrary, I could give you the names of people who were saved from torture and death because Don Jorge stood up for them."

The Argentine human-rights activist Adolfo Perez Esquivel, who won the 1980 Nobel Peace Prize, defended the new Pope against the accusation that he had taken an ambiguous attitude toward the military government. "There were bishops who were accomplices of the dictatorship, but Bergoglio was not one of them," he told a BBC interviewer. "Many religious people asked the military to pardon and release detainees, but achieved nothing." Bergoglio was among these clerics, Esquivel said. He said that those who were active with him in the struggle to protect human rights knew that there was no connection between the regime and Bergoglio—even if the archbishop was not fully prepared "to accompany our struggle for human rights." Graciela Fernandez Meijide, a former government minister who belonged to a commission investigating human-rights violations after the transition to democracy, said that the name Bergoglio never came up during their inquiries.

The Brazilian liberation theologian Leonardo Boff also jumped to the defense of the new Pope, saying that Bergoglio had "saved and hidden many who were persecuted by the military dictatorship." Boff's testimony is particularly interesting because of his history of conflict with the Church hierarchy. As a Franciscan priest, Father Boff was sentenced to penitential silence because of controversial statements in his writing. Angered by the condemnation of his work—which was signed by Cardinal Joseph Ratzinger, the future

Church of the Virgin Mary of Capuche in the *favela* (slum) Villa 21 in Buenos Aires. Archbishop Bergoglio took the bus to celebrate Mass with the people here.

Undated photo of a church service in the Barracas *favela*.

Communion service in the Barracas *favela* on December 8, 2012.

At Santa Francisca Javiera Cabrini Church
in Buenos Aires, November 7 2004.

Greeting the people after Mass,
March 21, 2011.

Pope Benedict XVI—Boff left the priesthood and the Franciscan order in the 1990s.
The new Pope is regarded as a friend of
the poor, but not a supporter of Liberation
Theology. So the testimony of Leonardo Boff
—a man who has no incentive to defend
Catholic prelates—carries special weight.

Several years ago, in *El Jesuita* and
in a magazine interview, Cardinal Bergoglio addressed the charges against him,
point by point. But he allowed that as
he looked back on his life: "The truth is
that I am a sinner, whom divine mercy
has treated particularly well . . . I have
committed so many mistakes that I cannot count them. Mistakes and sins."

In September of the Holy Year 2000,
all the Argentine bishops, acting on the
initiative of Archbishop Bergoglio, released a formal apology, a *mea culpa*, for
the attitude that many Church leaders
had taken toward the military regime:

"We were too tolerant of totalitarian
policies that violated democratic freedom
and respect for human dignity. Through
acts or omissions, we did fail to stand by
many of our brothers and sisters and did
not do enough to defend their rights. We
ask God, the Lord of history, to accept our
repentance and to heal the wounds of our
people. Oh Father, in your presence we
have to recall these dramatic and cruel
deeds! We ask your forgiveness for the
silence of those responsible and for those
of your children who have participated in
the political confrontation by violating freedom, by torturing and spying, through political persecution and ideological zealotry."

With their *mea culpa* the Argentine
bishops were following the lead of Blessed
John Paul II, who had called for a "purifi-
cation of memory," an internal cleansing
for the Church entering the new millen-
nium. On March 12, 2000, Pope John
Paul organized a dramatic ceremony in St.

Maundy Thursday liturgy 2008. Cardinal Bergoglio washes the feet of young drug addicts.

Peter's Basilica, asking God's forgiveness for the sins and faults of Church representatives throughout history.

"We are part of our nation," observed Archbishop Bergoglio after the bishops' statement was issued. "We can only proclaim that God gives himself to us freely if we have experienced this giving in the forgiveness of our sins." With a note of pride he compared the bishops' willingness to apologize for their failures with the silence of other institutions regarding their actions and inactions during the era of dictatorship. "No other sector in Argentine society has asked for forgiveness in this way," he observed.

In an interesting footnote to this historical era, it is possible that the first martyr proclaimed by Pope Francis could be a priest who was brutally murdered by the military regime in 1976. The Franciscan Father Murias Carlos was abducted from the village of El Chamical and tortured at a military base; his dead body was discovered in a field, with his eyes and hands missing. Cardinal Bergoglio opened the process of his cause for beatification in Mary 2011—doing so discreetly, noted a Franciscan provincial, to avoid provoking a reaction from other

Argentine bishops who had resented the murdered priest's social activism.

Liberation theology

Along with the tensions involved in relations with the military dictatorship, Father Bergoglio faced other difficulties during his tenure as Jesuit provincial in Argentina. Trouble was brewing within the Jesuit order itself. A substantial number of Jesuits were waving the banners of Liberation Theology, insisting that they should stand with the poor and the outcasts even to the point of political struggle. Father Bergoglio was skeptical. He fully supported the idea that the Church should serve the poor, but did not believe that priests and religious should play the role of political activists.

Conversation with young people at the Communion Mass of Maundy Thursday 2008.

Proponents of liberation theology saw Father Bergoglio then—and still regard him today—as a "complex and ambivalent personality," in the words of Martha Zechmeister, who teaches at the Jesuit university in El Salvador. On the one hand he "vigorously supports the marginalized and the exploited," and shows the courage to act on his beliefs. On the other hand, Zechmeister says, he has a "very conservative theological background and a rather authoritarian self-understanding." In *El Jesuita*, Cardinal Bergoglio said very little about liberation theology, mentioning only that he saw "good and bad aspects" of the teaching. He did make the observation, however, that the risk of "ideological infiltration" into the Church decreases when "the Church's awareness of the richness of popular piety grows." He seemed to be indicating that in a prayerful, unified Church, work for the poor would proceed without the taint of partisan politics or alien ideology.

As for "authoritarian self-awareness," it is true that Jorge Bergoglio had been attracted to the quasi-military structure of the Society of Jesus. As a provincial, he sought to be clear in his statements and disciplinary actions. He thereby rattled some cages within the Argentine Jesuit province. "You either loved him or you rejected him, there was nothing in between," said Jesuits who experienced Father Bergoglio's leadership. After six years at the helm he was not re-elected as provincial. Critics say that he left behind him a serious rift within the province; his defenders say that he did his best to contain the damage done by a split that had already occurred.

Some years later the head of the German bishops' relief organization, Misereor, saw then-Cardinal Bergoglio in action, and detected no hostility toward social activism. Joseph Sayer, who then represented the German bishops' humanitarian efforts in Latin America, attended the meeting of the Latin American bishops at the Marian shrine in Aparecida, Brazil in 2007.

Nobel Peace Prize winner Adolfo Perez Esquivel leaves the Spanish National Court in Madrid, Spain, Monday, Feb. 21, 2005, after testifying in a trial against an ex-Argentine navy officer accused of genocide committed in his country's "dirty war" more than two decades ago. (AP/Mariana Eliano)

"Right at the beginning Bergoglio was elected head of the editorial board, which is responsible for the final document, and thus for a ten-year program of the Church in Latin America," Sayer recalled in an interview with *Berliner Zeitung* after the new Pope's election. "That was a clear sign of confidence from his brethren." He quickly realized that Cardinal Bergoglio "listened to others, absorbed their opinions and positions and consolidated them for the good of the whole."

There was no trace of an authoritarian approach in his dealings with other prelates.

The meeting at Aparecida, guided in large part by Cardinal Bergoglio, deliberately chose a three-step approach—"See-Judge-Act"—to guide the work of the Church in Latin America. Some conservative bishops objected to that approach, and argued instead for a statement that would begin by setting forth principles of Catholic doctrine and then working from those principles to practical actions. Cardinal Bergoglio and his allies took the opposite point of view. They argued successfully that Church leaders should begin by analyzing the situation in their society, most notably including the impoverished plight of so many people in Latin America. Then the Church should weigh the situation in the light of Gospel teaching, and finally make recommendations for Church pastoral activity.

Joseph Sayer, the German bishops' representative at Aparecida, reports that he heard from the mouth of the future pontiff "the most severe condemnation of the neo-liberal economic model that I have ever heard." The Argentine cardinal complained that the poor are not only marginalized and excluded by the economic system, but actually treated as "waste." That statement, with its unblinking condemnation of inequality and injustice, echoes the tone of the final document approved by the Latin American bishops at Aparecida.

Sudden rise

As the 1970s came to a close, Father Jorge Mario Bergoglio was not a leading figure in Argentine society. He had made no memorable public speeches. He had been forced to step down as Jesuit provincial. He became a professor of theology, a rector, and a parish priest. In the 1980s—as Argentina went to war with Great Britain over the Falkland Islands, Pope John Paul II visited the country, and democratic rule was restored—Father Bergoglio was nearly hidden from the public eye. It was Pope John Paul II who ended this quiet interlude, granting the request of Cardinal Antonio Quarracino to appoint Father Bergoglio as an auxiliary bishop of Buenos Aires in 1992. In June of that year Cardinal Quarracino was the principal consecrator of Bishop Bergoglio, in a ceremony that took place in the cathedral of Buenos Aires.

In 2001, at a meeting of the Synod of Bishops in Rome, Jorge Mario Bergoglio—by then the Cardinal-Archbishop of Buenos Aires—outlined the requirements of a bishop's role: "A man of prayer. Called to be a saint. Poor for the sake of the Kingdom of God, like Jesus. Ordained, not only for service in his designated diocese,

but for the salvation of all people." These high standards actually reflected the summary of the Synod's discussions, but the chapter titles clearly show the Argentine cardinal's influence, and his understanding of his own episcopal ministry.

Five years after his episcopal ordination, Pope John Paul elevated the bishop to the rank of coadjutor with the right of succession, meaning that Bergoglio would become the Archbishop of Buenos Aires and Primate of Argentina upon Cardinal Quarracino's departure from office. A short nine months later Cardinal Quarracino died. Little Jorge, who had played on the sidewalks of the Flores neighborhood with Amalia, became the Archbishop of Buenos Aires in February 1998. Three years later he was raised to the College of Cardinals by the same Pope John Paul II.

Interestingly enough, Pope John Paul II, who was not considered a great friend of the Jesuit order, set two Jesuits at the head of two of the world's largest archdiocese: Bergoglio in Buenos Aires and Carlo Maria Martini, a noted biblical scholar, in Milan, the largest archdiocese in Europe. The two Jesuit cardinals became important figures in the papal conclave of 2005, according to reports that leaked out of the cardinals' deliberations. That conclave elected Pope Benedict XVI, and Cardinal Martini died in August 2012. But when Pope Benedict stepped down in February 2013, to the surprise of the general public Cardinal Bergoglio became pope after all.

An anti-clerical environment

As head of the Buenos Aires archdiocese, Cardinal Bergoglio soon emerged as a very important public figure, and everyone knew where he stood. President Néstor Kirchner saw him alternatively as the "secret leader of the opposition" or, more ominously, "a devil in robes." Both Kirchner and his wife Cristina, who succeeded him to the presidency after Néstor's death in 2010, avoided going to the cathedral after May 25, 2005, when the cardinal preached a powerful sermon in defense of society's outcasts and against the arrogance of power. The Kirchners felt that the preacher's remarks had been aimed at them personally. "You have to fight poverty, not the poor!" the cardinal said. He was not abusive, but tried to capture the attention of the congregation with a new approach. To hold a mirror up to a discredited elite, he chose the example of Zaccheus, the tax collector, from the Gospel. Zaccheus was corrupt and debauched, but when he heard that Jesus was coming he climbed a tree to have a clear view of him. Imitate Zaccheus, the cardinal suggested to his people. Climb up a tree, and let Jesus do the rest.

Leonardo Boff.

"In mid-November, the bishops of Argentina wanted to elect him as chairman of their Episcopal Conference but he refused," the Italian magazine *L'Espresso* reported late in 2002. Three years later Cardinal Bergoglio accepted the office, and he held it until 2011. Through those years he led the fight against permissive laws on drug possession, against legalized abortion, and against recognition of same-sex marriage. At the same time he spoke out repeatedly in defense of the poor and the marginalized. His voice was clear and his passion was intense, as in one homily when he cried out that "hundreds of children are disappearing and are sold as fresh meat. We beseech heaven that that does not happen to our family! There are wolves that rob our children who exploit them and force them into prostitution." In 2009 he set up a new post in the Buenos Aires archdiocese, appointing a vicar to supervise pastoral care in the *favelas*, the city's slums, because "society is

Pontifical Mass with pilgrims in front of the
Basilica of the Virgin of Luján, patron of
Argentina, on October 5, 2008.

cruel and only sees what it wants to see, and would prefer to erase the face of the poor."

"God lives in the city," the cardinal said in a speech in August 2011. He continued:

"He does not discriminate. His truth is one of encounter in which we look into each other's face, and each face is unique. Accepting people with their own faces, for their own sakes, does not entail a judgment of values. Only the look of love neither discriminates nor judges."

Cardinal Bergoglio's name popped up eight times in the confidential cables from the U.S. State Department that became public in the "Wikileaks" affair. The archbishop was seen by American diplomats as an important counterweight to the Kirchner regime. In cables to Washington, U.S. representatives in Argentina said that the cardinal was "concerned about the concentration of power in [Néstor] Kirchner's hands and the weakening of democratic institutions in Argentina." It was the cardinal's idea, according to the Wikileaks cables, to recruit a well-known Muslim as a parliamentary candidate for the opposition party. However, while these confidential reports claimed insights into the thinking of Cardinal Bergoglio, there was no evidence that he had any direct meetings with U.S. diplomats.

"He's shy," wrote *L'Espresso*, although also

straightforward. The Italian journal saw him as a man who did nothing to advertise himself—yet recognized that this was also one of his greatest strengths. Following his term as Jesuit provincial, *L'Espresso* reported that he had deliberately "stepped into the shadows, where Cardinal Quarracino had to literally fish him out." He nearly always declined requests for interviews, suggesting that reporters should draw material from his homilies and public statements—as if they could not possibly find anything

Undated photo of Archbishop Bergoglio.

of interest in him personally. When he was named a cardinal, he did not want a large delegation to accompany him to Rome for the ceremony in which he would receive his red hat. "Stay at home and give the money instead to those who need it," he pleaded.

With his simple style, and with his *mea culpa* for the failures of Church leaders during the years of the dictatorship, Cardinal Bergoglio won back respect for the Church in a society that had grown increasingly anticlerical. The "Mothers of the Plaza de Mayo," who could not forgive the hierarchy for its silence and even its complicity with the military regime, regarded the Archbishop of Buenos Aires with respect. Actually the cardinal showed that he had

his own complaints about some aspects of clerical life. "He has had his own personal difficulties with the Church environment," reported *L'Espresso*. In *El Jesuita* the cardinal remarked that it was "just fine" that many people believed in God but did not believe in priests. "Many of us priests do not deserve your trust," he said.

"Please, not to the Curia!"

The cardinal always wanted to be available to his priests, ready to help them with their needs. He gave pastors his phone number, telling them: "Call any time, if you have something on your mind." He declined to appoint a secretary, saying that he could put his schedule together for himself. For baptisms and confirmation ceremonies he rolled up to churches in a city bus. Often this priest, who had heard his calling to the ministry during a confession, would sit in a confessional like any other ordinary priest. When Jeronimo Podesta, a Catholic bishop who had abandoned the priesthood to marry, lay dying, Cardinal Bergoglio was the only current member of the Argentine hierarchy to visit him on his deathbed.

One could not be indifferent to Cardinal Bergoglio, said José Maria Poirier

After a major fire in a disco in the Argentine capital in January 2005, the cardinal celebrated a Mass in the cathedral for the victims and spoke with their families.

30,000 people live in the Villa 21 *favela*, where Cardinal Bergoglio was a frequent visitor.

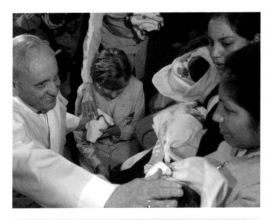

Blessing a baby after a Mass in Buenos Aires.

of the Catholic magazine *Criterio*. "He was always a man on the brink. Or on the border, as he himself more aptly put it. Keeping the same distances from liberation theology as from Opus Dei." Some saw him as a reactionary, others as a revolutionary. "It's very hard to define him," said Poirier. "He has held the bishops together through trying years, but both within the Jesuit community and within the Church of Argentina, he is either loved or hated—nothing in between."

The cardinal maintained good working contacts with Protestant groups in Argentina, and excellent relations with the Jewish community. In November 2012 he issued an open invitation to commemorate *Kristallnacht* in the cathedral in Buenos Aires, and he asked for "forgiveness for the sin of not having cared about the fate of our own brethren." On the same occasion he criticized the U.S. in unmistakable terms for failing to bomb the train lines leading into Auschwitz, saying that the decision was driven by "political opportunism, although they had the means" to stop the trains. Last year Cardinal Bergoglio took part in prayer services at a synagogue and a mosque, and invited Jewish and Muslim representatives to services at the cathedral.

International travel was not high on the cardinal's agenda. He had made his first trip abroad, to Colombia, in 1970. By the time he became a cardinal he had seen only a few places in Europe, apart from Italy. Once when he learned that

he was being considered for a post at the Vatican, he declined immediately. "Please, not to the Curia," he said, "or I shall die."

Benedict XVI in the consistory Hall in the Vatican, February 17, 2007, with Latin American bishops.

S till, for his duties as a cardinal he was required to attend a few meetings in Rome each year. Every time, he would book inexpensive airline tickets and wait calmly by himself at the baggage carousel until his luggage appeared. He once reported being very disappointed by a self-important man who expressed annoyance about waiting for his suitcase. "This made me very sad, to see someone who was so successful, failing at something so significant," he said. At the baggage carousel, he reflected, "we are all the same."

With Eliza (9) and Angela (12) at the Church of the Virgin Mary of Caapuche, Easter 2000.

W hen he arrived in Rome, Cardinal Bergoglio did not go directly to the Vatican, but checked into a modest clerical guest house near the Pantheon, where bed and breakfast cost 60 euros. When time was available he would make a side trip to Turin, where a cousin lived. Incidentally that same cousin had sewed his red cardinal's robes, because Bergoglio did not want to spend the 6,000 euros the vestments usually cost. ("No one has noticed the difference," he reports.) "My cousin is capable of blowing up the Vatican," says the seamstress, Giuseppina Rave Done Martinengo. "He is someone who revolutionizes everything, who is capable of giving everything to the poor."

In a crisis, turning to the Catechism

In 1998 Argentina slid into a severe economic crisis, which in some respects anticipated the worldwide financial crash that would occur four years later. Productivity plummeted. National leaders came and went. The government declared bankruptcy and devalued the currency. At the beginning of 2002—still prior to the worldwide crisis—banks were ordered closed for several days. Long before that, nearly 30 people died in riots that broke out in the wake of demonstrations in the center of Buenos Aires.

Demonstrators from the middle class, who suddenly found themselves left with nothing, signaled their demand for change by banging on cooking pots with ladles and spoons, creating an ear-splitting din. The Archbishop of Buenos Aires heard the cacophony from the *cacerolazos* (casserole pans); he knew that the Church had to respond.

But the Argentine bishops did not write a pastoral letter condemning capitalism, foreign debt, globalization, inequality, or the arrogant elite, as one might have expected. Nor did they launch an appeal for charity programs or a campaign for social justice. Instead—in a letter devoid of emotion and rancor, clearly showing the Bergoglio influence—they recommended that the people of Argentina now reach for their Catechisms, remember the Ten Commandments, and meditate on the Beatitudes. In a desperate situation, it was a highly unusual sort of recommendation.

"We present the message of the Catechism as it is," said the Archbishop of Buenos Aires:

"Anyone who follows it saves himself and the others. The sufferings of our people are clear: Many children are malnourished, and the hospitals lack the essentials for basic patient care. In this situation, the message of Jesus Christ is present to show the path he has prepared for us. To preserve dignity in his dignity. Everyone in our nation has a right to have their dignity respected and not trampled. To trample on the dignity of a woman, a man, a child or old man is a grave sin that cries out to heaven."

Wielding the Catechism as a weapon of reform in a time of crisis might at first glance seem naïve. But this recommendation shows the style of Bergoglio: a combination of simplicity and subtlety, fighting for the poor while trusting in God.

But the new Pope is not likely simply to press the Catechism of the Catholic Church into the hands of world leaders who visit him at the Vatican. More likely he will tell them something like what he told the magazine *30 Days* after the pastoral letter on the Catechism. The Argentine crisis was essentially a moral crisis, he explained, involving "the waste of taxpayers' money, an extreme liberalism coupled with the tyranny of the market, tax evasion, a lack of respect for law and order by citizens as well as by government, loss of the meaning of work; in short, corruption in general."

"Veritable economic and financial terrorism," the cardinal said, had "dramatically reduced the middle class and let the number of people in poverty swell." Because of a simultaneous collapse in education and training, there were 2 million young people in Buenos Aires who were neither students nor workers.

Cardinal Bergoglio saw too many people "idolizing money," and the situation reminded him of the golden calf in the Book of Exodus. "Where idols are worshipped, God and the dignity of man, made in God's image, are simultaneously erased."

Despite their difficult relationship, Cardinal Bergoglio and President Cristina Kirchner come together, March 18, 2010.

He spoke with distaste about a "speculation economy," which "does not even need more work, they do not know what to do with work." Still, he said, Latin America had "religious and spiritual resources" that could overcome the corruption of political and economic systems. Those resources could be found in the "simplicity of faith" of so many people in Latin America. He said:

"The Christian experience is not ideological. It is original. It comes from the

Cardinal Bergoglio signs a petition of world religious leaders denouncing terrorism and calling for peaceful co-existence, August 9, 2005.

December 12, 2012: Archbishop Bergoglio lights the Chanukah menorah with friends Rabbi Sergio Bergman (l) and Rabbi Alejandro Avruj (r).

miracle of encountering Jesus Christ, from the contemplation of the person of Jesus Christ."

The miracle of an encounter: These were the same words the new Pope had used to describe his vocational call to the priesthood in September 1953.

Cardinal Bergoglio did not want to offer economic or political recipes to ease the crisis in Argentina a decade ago, and Pope Francis is unlikely to offer such recipes to the world today. This is not the role of the Church, he says, because the Church is "not a lobby, not a pressure group." Still, in his interview with *30 Days* he had nothing good to say about the international economic leadership and major financial institutions. "To me it does not look as if they would actually put people at the center of their thinking, despite all their beautiful words," he said.

A parish church can organize hot meals for children and serve the growing ranks of the homeless, the cardinal said. "But we are sick of systems that produce poverty, leaving the poor to be tended to by the Church." The function of the political system should be to care for those who are most vulnerable, he said, and society must "rediscover the importance of politics as one of the highest forms of brotherly love."

At the end of the *30 Days* interview, when his questioner asked him how the crisis in Argentina would end, Cardinal Bergoglio suddenly shifted out of his gloomy perspective into the light. "I believe in miracles," he said. "Argentines are a big, beautiful people. The spiritual resources that they have are already a starting point for a miracle." Citing the words of Manzoni, he said, "The Lord never begins a miracle that He is not going to finish." The cardinal concluded: "I expect that everything will turn out well."

Fr. Gustavo Larrazabal, an Argentine Claretian missionary, has been the publisher of the books of Cardinal Bergoglio, now Pope Francis, during all his years as Archbishop of Buenos Aires.

his sermons and letters and edit them for publication, as a final record of his public statements as archbishop. That book was produced by the Claretian Publishing Group as *Open Mind, Believing Heart,* and became a popular work on Catholic spirituality. Father Gustavo Larrazabal, the publisher, recalls submitting the book's cover design to the cardinal. The cover featured a large, smiling image of Cardinal Bergoglio. "I sent it to him and told him that he was not going to like it, because his face was very visible," Father Larrazabal said. The cardinal approved the cover—not because he liked it but because he accepted the publisher's judgment.

Ready for retirement

On December 17, 2011, Cardinal Bergoglio celebrated his 75th birthday, and in accordance with Church law he submitted his resignation to Pope Benedict XVI. It is not uncommon for a Pope to ignore a resignation for months or even a few years, leaving a good bishop in place beyond the normal retirement age. So Cardinal Bergoglio remained at the helm in the Buenos Aires archdiocese.

However, the cardinal was preparing for his exit. He asked a priest to collect

Father Larrazabal, who had worked with Cardinal Bergoglio on other books and become a close friend, had developed much more than the ordinary publisher's relationship with an author:

I found in him a father and a friend whenever I had to go to him; a person who always heard me, together we could

A cup of mate tea during a visit to the *favela*, March 3, 2013 shortly before the papal elections.

find solutions; a person always optimistic, but not naively optimistic. He is, without doubt, a man of great faith and much prayer. His advice was always qualified, as of a spiritual guide: advising, guiding . . . I don't know how to explain it, but after talking with him, you would have another perspective to address the problem.

When *Open Mind, Believing Heart* appeared in Argentine bookstores, the publisher recalls, Cardinal Bergoglio "told us that it was going to be his last work as Archbishop of Buenos Aires." And so it was—but not for the reason the author expected.

The 2005 conclave

According to many published accounts, Cardinal Bergoglio won as many
as 40 votes in the conclave of 2005,
emerging as the leading alternative to
Cardinal Joseph Ratzinger before the
latter was elected as Pope Benedict XVI.
The Argentine prelate himself refused
to comment on reports about the 2005
votes, saying that he was "confused and a
bit hurt" by the knowledge that someone
had violated the secrecy of the conclave.

Although some observers at that
time saw Cardinal Bergoglio as a "liberal"
alternative to the "conservative" Cardinal
Ratzinger, the Argentine prelate did not
fit easily into a liberal mold. He had been
firm in his defense of Church teachings on
controversial issues such as abortion and
homosexuality, drawing the ire of political
radicals in Argentina. He had distanced
himself from fellow Jesuits who promoted
a leftist political agenda, and shown strong
sympathy for the Communion and Liberation movement in Argentina. Nevertheless the new pontiff had shown an ability
to draw support from different corners
of the Catholic world. He was known for
his personal humility, which was mani-
fested in his decision to ride buses, live
in a spare apartment, and make his own
meals. He had a deep commitment to
helping the poor, and a passion for evangelization. He was, in short, an attractive
candidate for the papacy, even in 2005.

Predecessor and successor: encountering Pope
Benedict XVI in Rome, January 13, 2007.

However, the conclave of 2005 was domi-
nated by a single question: Would the electors choose Cardinal Ratzinger, who was
clearly the dominant personality in their
midst? Some cardinals apparently resisted,
perhaps concerned about the German prelate's age, or his reputation for doctrinal
rigor. For these prelates, the quiet cardinal
from Argentina emerged as a likely alternative. But ultimately the resistance collapsed
and the conclave said "Yes" to Ratzinger.

Andrea Ricciardi, the founder of the
influential Sant'Egidio community in Rome,
recalls encounters with Cardinal Bergoglio
before and after the election of Benedict XVI:

"I saw him pray, alone, in a church in
Rome before the conclave of 2005, which
led to the election of Benedict XVI. I saw
him again praying alone in the church,
after the conclave, during which he had received a high number of votes. I remember
his smile and the words he said to me: 'It
is not the time for a non-European pope.'"

Series of Surprises

"How I wish for a Church that is poor, and for the poor!" With statements like that—made to reporters at the first public audience of his pontificate—Pope Francis let the world know that this new pontiff would bring a different perspective to the Vatican. In his first few days as pope he provided a curious world with a number of news stories about this interesting new pontiff who stopped to pet dogs, paid his own hotel bill, quoted Hölderlin from memory, and made himself available after Mass outside the door of the parish church, just like any other priest, to greet the faithful. This surprising new Pope raised many different expectations among the faithful. Could he possibly fulfill them all?

Paying his own tab

Less than 24 hours after his election, Pope Francis had caused his first sensation. He quietly slipped out of the Vatican, traveling without any prior announcement in a plain black sedan, to visit the basilica of St. Mary Major. He was doing what he had promised the crowd in St. Peter's square after his election: "Tomorrow I want to go to pray to the Madonna, that she may protect Rome."

St. Mary Major is the oldest church in Rome dedicated to the Virgin, and the most prominent, so it was a natural choice for the pope's short pilgrimage. It is also a church that draws thousands of visitors every day, and Pope Francis told Vatican aides that he did not want his own visit to interfere with others; he wanted to be "a pilgrim among the pilgrims." That desire was thwarted by Vatican security officials, who restricted access to the basilica during the Pope's visit.

Entering the basilica, he laid a bouquet before the *Salus Populi Romani* ("the salvation of the people of Rome"), an ancient icon depicting the Virgin Mary that was painted, according to pious tradition, by St. Luke the evangelist. Pope Francis was underlining the message that he had sent in his earliest words to the public, confirming that he was first and foremost the Bishop of Rome.

Flowers for the Madonna: on the first morning after his election, Pope Francis visits the basilica of Saint Mary Major.

Next the pontiff visited a chapel in the basilica where St. Ignatius of Loyola, the founder of the Jesuit order, celebrated his first Mass. Thus he sent another message: he was not forgetting his Jesuit heritage. Finally the Pope stopped again to pray at the tomb of St. Pius V. It was probably no coincidence that Pius V is remembered for his firm opposition to a rising tide of Islamic power and for attacking corruption in the Church. These were precisely the problems that Francis would now face.

On his trip to St. Mary Major the Pope was accompanied by Archbishop Georg Gänswein, the prefect of the pontifical household, who had been private secretary to Pope Benedict XVI. The Argentine prelate did not have his own priest-secretary; he was unaccustomed to having an aide constantly at his side. He left the basilica by a side door, waving to a group of students who were surprised to see the pontiff appearing unannounced in the middle of the city.

Before returning to the Vatican the Pope made another stop at the guest house near the Pantheon where he had been staying before the conclave. He explained that he needed to "pick up a few things," then stunned the staff by appearing at the front desk to pay the bill for his lodging. For a Roman pontiff this was sensational behavior: to pick up his own bags, to pay his own bill! The staff of the

His deep love for the Mother of God led Pope Francis immediately to the Lourdes grotto in the Vatican Gardens.

pontifical household usually handles all such details for the pope. But obviously Pope Francis wanted to continue to live simply, to do his own menial work, with the humility that the name of "Francis" evokes. In making his trip around Rome, first to the basilica and then to the clerical guest house, without advance planning, he was also acting with a spontaneity that is not often allowed to Roman pontiffs. Even while they found his actions refreshing, many observers wondered whether the new Pope would be able to continue acting this way, as the pressures of his schedule and the weight of Vatican traditions began to press upon him.

Just picking up a few things: Pope Francis stops to pay the bill at the guest house where he stayed before the conclave.

Those questions arose later on Thursday, the first full day of the new pontificate, as the Pope returned to the Sistine Chapel to celebrate Mass with the cardinals who had elected him. The long line of prelates, all dressed in the same vestments, solemnly approached the altar in procession, while the Sistine Chapel choir sang *Tu Es Petrus*. In this chapel with its spectacular Renaissance art, the scene had a timeless quality; nothing seemed new. The Pope himself, no longer a young man at 76, walked with a slight limp. How long could he continue rushing around the city? How could he continue living like a mendicant, in these imposing palaces, surrounded by the works of Michelangelo, Perugino, and Raphael?

Still the Pope's new style did become evident, even in this ceremony. He celebrated Mass facing the congregation, using a plywood altar temporarily set up in front of the Last Judgment fresco. He delivered his homily from the ambo, in Italian rather than Latin, without wearing his miter. These were all minor details, but in the Vatican such details are watched carefully, and for countless Catholics seeking to learn more about their new pontiff the details were important.

In that six-minute homily, which he delivered without a prepared text, the Pope told the cardinals that the Church of Christ cannot stand still. "Our life is a path," he said. "When we stop walking, there is something that isn't right." A priest especially, he continued, must avoid the temptation to become "a religious functionary." He emphasized that the Church must be active, always seeking to help people. However, he continued, the Church must offer a particular sort of help. "We can build many things, but if we do not witness to Jesus Christ then it doesn't matter. We might become a philanthropic NGO but we wouldn't be the Church, the Bride of the Lord."

The Church will always face obstacles in this work, the Pope said. Good priests will not be deterred, but will accept difficulties as a means of sharing in the sufferings of Jesus Christ. He said that "when we walk without the Cross, when we build without the Cross, when we profess a Christ without the Cross . . . we aren't disciples of the Lord." The pontiff warned the cardinals what results when clerics do not embrace the Cross: "We are worldly. We are bishops, priests, cardinals, popes, but not disciples of the Lord."

The Pope's first homily was a stern warning against the secularization of the Church. His style was very different, but the substance of his message was very similar to a theme that Benedict XVI had sounded many times before. There would be dramatic changes in this pontificate, it seemed; but there would be continuity as well.

"A changed man?"

On Friday another scene unfolded in which everything seemed to be just as it was, except for the unusual character of the new Pope. In the stately Clementine Hall of the apostolic palace, Francis met with the members of the College of Cardinals—this time including those who, by reason of age, had not participated in the conclave. The setting was the same as it had been when Pope Benedict XVI held his last meeting with his cardinals before his resignation took effect. Cardinal Angelo Sodano offered a similar greeting and expression of loyalty. The cardinals sat, silent and attentive, as they had before. But the Pope was different.

This time Pope Francis spoke from a prepared text. His delivery was less energetic, and some passages of his address sounded unlike his own prose style: "In these days we felt, almost tangibly, the affection and solidarity of the universal Church, as well as the attention of many people who, although they do not share our faith, look to the Church and the Holy See with respect and admiration." Already the pope seemed to be bowing to the reality of his new position. A Roman pontiff must deliver many formal statements, and needs helping draft them. The smooth, seamless style of the Roman Curia was evident in this talk.

But the style of Pope Francis shone through as well. A speechwriter may have helped with the text, but the substance of

Pope Francis, who avoided interviews during his tenure in Buenos Aires, meets with media representatives.

ry day," Pope Francis said. He expressed his full confidence that the world of the 21st century would listen to the Christian message, because "it responds to the deepest needs of human existence." The Pope concluded his talk by encouraging the cardinals to bring the prayerful spirit of the conclave back to their own dioceses: "Now return to your sees to continue your ministry enriched by the experience of these days that have been so full of faith and ecclesial communion." Quoting from "a German poet" (he was referring to Friedrich Hölderlin), he said of old age, *"Es ist ruhig das Alter, und fromm"* ("It is a time of peace and of prayer").

During these first few days of the pontificate, as Vatican officials introduced Francis to the workings of the Vatican, the new pope showed a remarkable ability to adapt to the ceremonial life of the Holy See, with all its history and symbolism, while making occasional symbolic statements of his own. When he toured the papal apartments in the apostolic palace, which had been sealed since the resignation of Benedict XVI, he

the address was distinctly his own, and the Pope could not restrain himself from adding several ad-lib remarks. "Probably half of us are in our old age," he remarked to the cardinals. But as old age brings greater understanding, he encouraged the prelates to "give wisdom to the youth: like good wine that improves with age, let us give the youth the wisdom of our lives."

"Let us never give in to pessimism, to that bitterness that the devil offers us eve-

> "A little bit of compassion makes the world less cold and more just."
>
> *Pope Francis in his homily*
> *at St. Ann's parish church on March 17, 2013*

expressed astonishment at their size, and decided to continue living in the far more modest suite of rooms that he was occupying in the Domus Sanctae Marthae, the Vatican's guest house, where he could be closer to the ordinary employees of the Vatican work force, and celebrate morning Mass with them each day.

Although the papal apartments are certainly spacious, the new pope's judgment that they were too large may have been colored by the fact that he did not have—and apparently did not plan to have—a small domestic staff living with him. Previous pontiffs shared the space with a few priest-secretaries. Pope Francis had no one filling that role. As he explored his new surroundings he was usually accompanied by Archbishop Gänswein, the private secretary of the previous pope, who now functioned as a sort of bridge between the two pontificates. Archbishop Gänswein was his *cicerone*, guiding him through the intricate world of the Vatican.

Respect for unbelievers

Archbishop Gänswein was seated at his side on Saturday, when he held the first public audience of his pontificate, hosting the more than 5,000 reporters in the Vatican's audience hall, the Nervi. He began by reminding the journalists that he, himself, was not really the story. "Christ is the center," he said. "Not the successor of Peter, but Christ." He continued:

"Christ is the foundation and reference point, the heart of the Church. Without him there would neither Peter nor the Church, nor would they have any reason to exist."

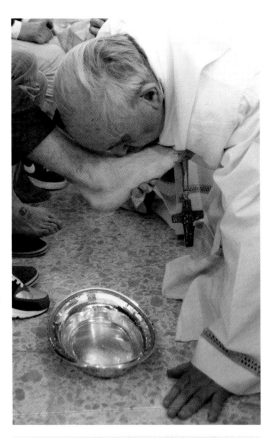

Francis washes the feet of a dozen residents at the Casal del Marmo, a juvenile detention center, on Holy Thursday. As archbishop he had often chosen to celebrate the Mass of the Lord's Supper in a prison, and he continued that pattern in Rome. Setting aside Church liturgical directives, he includes two young women, as well as Muslim inmates, among those whose feet he washes in the ritual, which recalls Christ's washing the feet of his apostles.

Once again the Pope had a prepared text, but in another display of his penchant for spontaneity, he set it aside to speak instead about how he had chosen the name "Francis." He disclosed that an old friend, the Brazilian Cardinal Claudio Hummes, had been seated next to him during the conclave, and bucked him up when the early ballots showed an alarming trend in his direction. When the fifth ballot gave Cardinal Bergoglio the two-thirds majority that was required, and the cardinals burst into applause, the pope recalled that Cardinal Clàudio Hummes gave him a congratulatory hug and a few words of advice: "Do not forget the poor." Those few words struck home, the Argentine pontiff said, and "immediately I thought of St. Francis of Assisi." St. Francis, he explained, was "a man of poverty, a man of peace, a man who loved Creation." He observed that at the moment, "We do not have a very good relationship with Creation, do we?"

After his remarks the Pope spent some time mingling with the journalists, greeting a few old friends and stooping to pat a reporter's guide dog. But before the audience ended he unleashed another surprise. Speaking in Spanish, a language that many of those in the audience did not understand, he said a few words into the microphone, stood silent for a moment, and then turned to leave the hall. An official Vatican translation later explained that the Pope had said he wanted to give the journalists his blessing. "But since many of you do not belong to the Catholic Church, and others are not believers, I will cordially impart this blessing to each of you in silence—with respect for the conscience of each individual, but in the knowledge that each one of you is a child of God. God bless you." So the Roman pontiff had decided not to trace the Sign of the Cross over the audience, out of respect for non-believers.

This punctilious respect for unbelievers may have been foreshadowed in the interviews with then-Cardinal Bergoglio that supplied the material for the book *El Jesuita*, in which the future pontiff spoke of how the work of Jorge Luis Borges had helped to shape his thought. Borges, a native of Argentina, was a giant of 20th century literature, a poet and short-story writer whose fantastic stories form the basis of the Latin American tradition of "magical realism." Although he was an agnostic, Borges was a writer who regularly explored spiritual and metaphysical themes, and peppered his work with themes from the Bible and the Christian tradition.

Cardinal Bergoglio had known Borges personally. While teaching literature classes in Santa Fe, he once traveled to Buenos Aires to show some of his students' short stories to the man known as Argentina's Homer. He even persuaded Borges to perform a reading of his works for a class in Santa Fe. "He was a very wise man," said the future pope—who recalled that the agnostic writer faithfully said an "Our Father" every night, because he had promised his mother he would do so. Borges never directly addressed the question of whether or not God exists, Cardinal Bergoglio observed. He was intrigued and edified by his conversations with the famous writer.

Jorge Luis Borges (1899–1986).

Meeting the people

The first Sunday of the Argentine papacy brought a series of "firsts"—his first Twitter message (reviving a practice that Benedict XVI had begun not long before his retirement), his first midday audience from the window of the apostolic palace, and his first papal Mass celebrated for a congregation of ordinary Catholics.

For that Mass the new Pope had chosen to visit the little parish church of St. Anne, just inside the gates of Vatican City. Promptly at 10:00 a.m. he appeared at the altar, wearing purple Lenten vestments, to celebrate Mass for a mixed community of Vatican employees, residents of the neighboring Borgo district, and a number of people who were

Neighbors from Buenos Aires bring letters for the Pope to his sister.

curious to see whether the Pope's Mass would be very different from the celebration in any other parish. It was not.

That Sunday's Gospel reading recounted the story of the woman caught in adultery. Reflecting on that incident in his homily, Pope Francis remarked that the same people who were prepared to stone that woman had probably heard Jesus preaching in the Temple, but had not accepted his message of love. "I also think that we are like these people, who on the one hand want to listen to Jesus, but on the other hand, at times, like to be cruel."

Pope Francis greeting the faithful after a Mass at Saint Anne's church on March 17.

Isn't that right?" the Pope challenged the congregation. Yet despite our capacity to be cruel, Pope Francis said, Jesus "has the special ability to forget." He exhorted the congregation: "Let us ask for the grace never to tire of asking for forgiveness."

When the Mass ended, the Pope greeted parishioners at the parish door. Then he made his way over toward St. Peter's Basilica. Hundreds of people had already begun to arrive there for his Angelus audience, and the Pope surprised them when he appeared in person at the gate on the Via di Porta Angelica and—to the obvious discomfort of his security detail—waded into the crowd to greet people personally.

That scene, in which the Pope mixed informally with passersby on the streets of Rome, had not been seen since the pontificate of John Paul I, who reigned in the fall of 1978 for just 33 days before his sudden death. The simplicity of Francis' preaching also reminded some observers of John Paul I. At the same time the stature and the gregarious nature of the new Pope was reminiscent of Blessed John XXIII, the stout son of a farmer from northern Italy who was considered a "transitional Pope" —a temporary caretaker—when he was elected, but surprised the Catholic world by convening the Second Vatican Council.

The faithful wave palm branches as Pope Francis celebrates Palm Sunday Mass in St. Peter's Square on March 24, 2013.

In 2000, Pope John Paul II had described John XXIII as "a shepherd who went out into the streets"—a description that would apparently fit Pope Francis as well. In *El Jesuita*, Cardinal Bergoglio had spoken with approval about the way Pope John, when he was Patriarch of Venice, would go to a café in St. Mark's Square before noon to have a glass of wine and chat with the people there. "That to me is a shepherd: someone who goes out to meet the people," said the Argentine cardinal.

The crowd for the Pope's first Sunday audience spilled out of St. Peter's

Square and down the Via della Concilia-zione toward the Castel Sant'Angelo and the Tiber. In his address the Pope again showed his simple, popular approach. *"Buon giorno!"* he began. He mentioned that he had recently read a new book by Cardinal Walter Kasper, "but don't think that I'm doing publicity for the cardinal's books, because I'm not." He returned to the theme of forgiveness that he had explored in his homily that morning, and recalled that he had once met an elderly woman who said, "If the Lord did not forgive everyone, the world would not exist." Commending her insight, the Pope

"wanted to ask her: 'Have you studied at the Gregorian?'" (The Gregorian, a Jesuit institution in the heart of Rome, is perhaps the most famous of the city's Catholic universities, a training ground for future theologians and bishops.) He ended his audience with a suggestion that any Roman could take to heart: "Have a good Sunday, and a good lunch."

The Pope told the crowd at his Angelus audience that he had chosen the name "Francis" in part because Francis of Assisi was the patron saint of Italy. "This reinforces my spiritual bond

Pope John XXIII as he left the Vatican by train on a pilgimage to Loreto and Assisi on October 8, 1962.

It was the desire to build a church, both literally and figuratively, that gave St. Francis the inspiration to begin his apostolic work. The son of a wealthy merchant, young Francis had cast off his expensive clothes as a sign of his commitment to poverty, when he experienced one of the most dramatic moments of a very eventful life. At prayer in the dilapidated church of San Damiano in the town of Assisi, the great saint heard the voice of Jesus saying, "Francis, rebuild my church, which you see is in ruins." St. Francis took that directive literally and began to repair the crumbling walls of San Damiano. But of course the message of Christ had a deeper meaning, calling for a spiritual renewal throughout the universal Church.

with the place—where, as you know, my family has its origins," he said.

"Rebuild my Church."

Between his Angelus audience and his remarks to journalists the previous day, the Pope had now provided a substantial list of reasons for choosing to be known as Francis: because Francis loved the poor, because he was a man of peace, because he respected Creation, because he came from Italy. These were all good reasons. But there was one reason conspicuously missing from the list: because St. Francis of Assisi made it his life's work to rebuild the Church.

Pope Francis had been elected at a time when many Catholics, and many Church leaders, recognized the need for a renewal, especially within the Vatican itself. The cardinals' conversations leading into the conclave had been marked by some tensions regarding the problems that had been exposed in the Roman Curia: the leaked correspondence, the squabbling, the public-relations blunders, and—far worse—the accusations of corruption. There was a general consensus, it seemed, that the new Pope would need to undertake a thorough reform of the Vatican bureaucracy. And beyond Rome, the universal Church was still suffering from the crushing effects of the sex-abuse scandal; a spiritual renewal of the priesthood in particular, and the Church in general, were sorely needed. In that context it is difficult to imagine that the Pope—who knew the story of St. Francis quite well—was not mindful of the mission to "rebuild my Church" when he took the saint's name.

Vatican-watchers were following the new Pope's moves carefully, trying to detect any sign of how Francis planned to handle the calls for reform of the Curia. For the first two days of the pontificate there were no hints at all. In a way even that was significant. When the Holy See becomes vacant, the terms of all the top officials in the Roman Curia lapse, since they hold authority only as representatives of the pontiff. Ordinarily a newly elected pope quickly renews their appointments; he may eventually replace some officials with his own choices, but he leaves the old prefects in place so that the ordinary work of the Vatican can resume. Pope Francis, however, waited for three days before saying that the Curial leaders should remain *donec aliter provideatur*—until other provisions are made.

That important proviso indicated that the new Pope does indeed plan to make changes in the administration of Vatican affairs, although it leaves open the question of what sort of changes. Journalists in Rome concluded that the Pope would soon begin to install his own team of carefully chosen aides. It seemed to be a foregone conclusion that he would replace Cardinal Tarcisio Bertone, the Secretary of State, who

Argentine Catholics gather at the cathedral in Buenos Aires, waiting for the start of a Mass to mark the beginning of the pontificate of their former archbishop, on March 19.

had, rightly or wrongly, been fixed with the lion's share of the blame for the disarray at the Vatican. The choice of his replacement would be one of the key early tests of the new pope's organizational abilities.

A call to home

Very early on Tuesday morning, March 19, Pope Francis placed an unexpected call to his native Argentina. In the main square of Buenos Aires, the Plaza de Mayo, a crowd had begun to gather well before dawn, to watch a broadcast of the Pope's inaugural Mass on a giant video monitor. The papal Mass would take place at 5:30 a.m. (Argentine time). Shortly after 3:30, the early arrivals heard a familiar voice over the sound system in the Plaza de Mayo, and exploded into excited applause. It was the man who, just a week earlier, had been their archbishop.

An Argentine newspaper explained how this extraordinary trans-Atlantic con-

Pope Francis, followed by Cardinal Angelo Comastri and Bishop Vittorio Lanzani (partially hidden) visits the crypt under St. Peter's Basilica, where St. Peter is buried, on April 1.

Fiesta Latinoamericana in St. Peter's Square.

versation had occurred. The Pope had called the rector of the city's cathedral, who had found a way to route the call into the sound system in the square nearby.

"I want to ask for us to walk together, to care for one another, for you to care for each other," the Pope told the delighted crowd. "Don't forget this bishop, who though far away, cares so much for you," the Pope said. "Pray for me," he requested, before giving the crowd his blessing.

A few days later the Pope placed an even more unusual call to Buenos Aires, to the proprietor of a little kiosk where he had picked up his newspaper every day. Pope Francis politely told his old friend—as if he needed to be told!—that he would no longer be stopping by the newsstand, and wanted to cancel his subscription. Again the Pope's simplicity, his spontaneity, and his common touch were disarming. The incident demonstrated that ordinary expectations about the workings of the papacy would have to change. Under the new regime, it seemed, anyone might receive a surprise phone call from the Pope!

Pope Francis was beginning to settle into his new routine at the Vatican. But he was not settling into the papal apartments. The Vatican press office disclosed that the Pope had decided to remain at the Domus Sanctae Marthae "for now." Renovations were still unfinished in the more formal apartments on the third floor of the apostolic palace, and they would be ready whenever the Pope chose to move there. But it was clear that he felt more comfortable where he already was. Perhaps he also felt that living outside the apostolic palace would give him more perspective on changes that might be needed in the offices there, in the pontifical household and the neighboring Secretariat of State.

In his unending quest for simplicity the Pope had already encountered his first critics: the practitioners of classical heraldry. The experts were appalled when they saw the design that the new Pope had approved for his official coat of arms, combining elements from his coat of arms as a bishop. Under a bishop's miter and crossed keys of Peter—copied from the coat of arms of Benedict XVI—the blue shield that Francis wanted showed the emblem of the Jesuit order, a circle with the initials "IHS," for Jesus Christ; a star representing Mary, and a spikenard flower for St. Joseph. Lovers of heraldry found the design crude, and protested that the spikenard was not a traditional symbol. They did not object, however, to the Pope's motto, displayed below the shield: *Miserando atque eligendo*. That motto, taken from a sermon by the Venerable Bede on the calling of St. Matthew, is not easily translated into English. *Miserando atque eligendo* means "to be pitied and yet chosen" and

refers to how Jesus called Matthew the tax collector. The Gospel of St. Matthew has a special place in the new Pope's heart. It was on the feast of St. Matthew, September 21, that the young Jorge Bergoglio had his unexpected "encounter" in a confessional in the Flores neighborhood, and realized that he was called to become a priest.

The inaugural Mass

Pope Francis formally began his pontificate that day, the Feast of St. Joseph, with a solemn Mass celebrated in St. Peter's Square. After teeming rain on Monday night, thousands of people began filtering into St. Peter's Square early in the morning to secure a place in the ceremony. But by the time the Mass began there was still some space remaining in the square, which holds about 250,000 people. Apparently some people had been deterred by the wet weather, or delayed by the tight security screening at the entrances to the Vatican. The area immediately in front of St. Peter's Basilica presented a colorful scene, with the scarlet vestments of the prelates, the white of the many concelebrating priests, the purple curtain at the entrance of the basilica, and the yellow-and-white canopies under which priests would distribute Communion.

In front of St. Peter's, seated according to protocol, were the representatives of 132 different nations and international organizations. Argentina's President Cristina

Rome's Chief Rabbi Riccardo Di Segni attending Pope Francis's inauguration Mass in St. Peter's Square.

Rabbi Riccardo Di Segni, the head of the Jewish community in Rome—to whom Francis had sent a message of greeting shortly after his election—was the first Jewish leader in memory to attend a pope's inaugural Mass. And the Orthodox Patriarch Bartholomew I of Constantinople, "first among equals" of all the world's Orthodox patriarchs, became the first Ecumenical Patriarch ever to attend the installation of a Roman pontiff. Later it emerged that the Orthodox prelate had invited Pope Francis to join him on a pilgrimage to Jerusalem in 2014, marking the 50th anniversary of the historic meeting there between their predecessors, Pope Paul VI and Patriarch Athenagoras, in the Holy City, which had been the first encounter between Pope and Ecumenical Patriarch since the Great Schism of 1054.

Kirchner, who had met with her country's first Pope in a friendly informal audience on Monday, was there. So was Zimbabwe's autocratic ruler, Robert Mugabe, whose many violations of human rights had been condemned by the country's Catholic hierarchy and made him persona non grata in the European Union. (Mugabe was able to travel to Rome only because the Holy See is not a member of the European Union.) The Vatican handled political questions about the guests carefully, saying that no one had been invited to the celebration, but everyone was welcome.

Among all the assembled dignitaries, two guests were particularly noteworthy.

The importance of Patriarch Bartholomew's appearance would be difficult to overstate. Commentators immediately pointed out that since the Great Schism, no Patriarch from Constantinople had attended the inauguration of a Bishop of Rome. That was true, but it was also an understatement. In 2,000 years of Christian history no Patriarch of Constantinople had ever attended such a ceremony. Relations between Rome and Constantinople had warmed significantly since the Second Vatican Council, and Bartholomew I had become a close friend of Benedict XVI. Still the Pope's repeated references to himself as the "Bishop of Rome" may have helped

Pope Francis meets Bartholomew I, the first Ecumenical Patriarch to attend the installation of a Pope since the Catholic and Orthodox churches split nearly 1,000 years ago.

to persuade the Orthodox prelate to take this important symbolic step. The Orthodox churches are quite ready to recognize the Pope as Bishop of Rome; it is the extent of his authority over the universal Church that causes debates in ecumenical gatherings.

Before the start of the Mass, the Pope arrived in the open-backed "popemobile," which made a few slow circles through St. Peter's Square, allowing the Pope to greet the crowd. At one point he dramatically had the vehicle stop and jumped out to embrace and give his blessing to a severely disabled man, speaking with him and with others nearby before he climbed back into the popemobile to continue his circuit.

The formal ceremony began with a procession into St. Peter's Basilica, where the Pope venerated the tomb of St. Peter, accompanied by the Ecumenical Patriarch. Then he was vested with the *pallium*, the symbol of his authority, placed over his shoulders by Cardinal Jean-Louis Tauran, the senior cardinal-deacon. Next he received the Fisherman's Ring, placed on his finger by Cardinal Angelo Sodano, dean of the College of Cardinals. In the final ritual confirming his new authority, he received acts of obedience from six cardinals who had been selected to repre-sent the entire College of Cardinals. The traditional rituals of a papal inauguration had been trimmed to accommodate the

People proudly wave their countries' flags during the inaugural Mass of the first pontiff from the New World.

U.S. Vice President Joseph Biden greets the new Pope after his inaugural Mass.

Pope Francis greets the Governor General of Canada, David Johnston, with his wife Sharon.

The Fisherman's Ring: sign of papal office.

Pope, who had asked for a simpler ceremony, saying that he did not want to overtax the endurance of a large congregation. At one point later in the ceremony, keen-eyed observers noticed that the Pope checked his watch, calculating whether the celebration would be completed within the two-hour framework he had set. It was.

In his homily the Pope again paid tribute to his predecessor, noting that the date was the patronal feast of Joseph Ratzinger. He went on to say that St. Joseph's mission in life was to protect Jesus and Mary. "Let us protect Christ in our lives, so that we can protect others,

so that we can protect creation," the Pope said. He went on:

"I would like to ask all those who have positions of responsibility in economic, political and social life, and all men and women of goodwill: let us be "protectors" of creation, protectors of God's plan inscribed in nature, protectors of one another and of the environment."

For the first time in his pontificate, Francis acknowledged in his homily that he, as Roman pontiff, held special universal authority in the Catholic Church. He quickly added, however, that "authentic power is service, and that the Pope too, when exercising power, must enter ever more fully into that service which has its radiant culmination on the Cross."

The "dictatorship of relativism"

After his inaugural Mass the Pope received the official national delegations that had attended the ceremony, and also received (as the dignitaries told reporters) a large number of invitations to visit their countries. Cristina Kirchner, after an encounter in which she and Pope Francis had done their best to bury their past differences, assured him that he would be eagerly awaited in his native land. Martin Schulz, the president of the European Parliament, asked him to deliver an address to that body. Chaldean Catholic Patriarch Louis Sako suggested a trip to troubled Iraq, to visit the birthplace of Abraham. Delegates from Colombia and Australia put in their bids for a papal visit. Even Zimbabwe's Robert Mugabe, whose presence made Vatican diplomats uneasy, expressed hope that the Pope would visit his country.

Only one of these many invitations was met with a directly positive response. Brazilian Cardinal Raymundo Damasceno Assis told reporters that he had been assured the Pope would attend the international celebration of World Youth Day, scheduled to take place in Rio de Janeiro in July. Brazilian President Dilma Rousseff began discussing some details of the projected papal trip during a March 20 meeting with the pontiff.

The round of official audiences still was not over. On March 20 the Pope met with representatives of other religious groups. In the Clementine Hall, the Pope made his first symbolic statement by taking his seat in an armchair, rather than the throne usually reserved for the pontiff. Orthodox Patriarch Bartholomew I welcomed the Pope on behalf of the other religious leaders, mentioning the Pope's "elevated, serious, and difficult task" of promoting unity among believers. Pope Francis replied by thanking "my brother Andrew"—referring to the Ecumenical Patriarch by using the name of the patron saint of Constantinople, just as Catholics often refer to the Pope as "Peter." He thanked all the religious leaders for the support they had shown by attending his inaugural ceremony.

"For my part, I wish to assure, following my predecessors, the firm wish to continue on the path of ecumenical dialogue," the Pope said to the Christian delegates. He also saluted representatives of the Jewish people, "to whom we are bound by a very special spiritual bond," and of Islam, promising that they would find the Holy See anxious to

cooperate in every endeavor that would promote the welfare of mankind.

The first meeting with the ambassadors to the Holy See from around the world.

One final important event remained on the Pope's list of introductory audiences: a March 22 audience with all the diplomats accredited to the Holy See, which would furnish the occasion for the Pope's first public address on the world's political affairs. In that talk the Pope again spoke about the importance of dialogue, particularly with Islam, reiterated his commitment to the effort to help people living in poverty. But the most important passage of his speech came when he

unmistakably affirmed a major theme of the previous pontificate, speaking out against the "tyranny of relativism, which makes everyone his own criterion and endangers the coexistence of peoples."

The Pope told the diplomats that when he chose to be known as Francis, he realized that the saint is "a familiar figure far beyond the borders of Italy and Europe, even among those who do not profess the Catholic faith." St. Francis can be a model to all people, not just to Christians, he said, because of his devotion to helping the poor.

"But there is another form of poverty," the Pope continued. "It is the spiritual poverty of our time, which afflicts the so-called richer countries particularly seriously." In that context he mentioned the "tyranny of relativism." While the quest for peace is a top priority, the pontiff cautioned:

"But there is no true peace without truth! There cannot be true peace if everyone is his own criterion, if everyone can always claim exclusively his own rights, without at the same time caring for the good of others, of everyone, on the basis of the nature that unites every human being on this earth."

Francis reminded his audience that the term "pontiff" refers to a "bridge-builder," and said that he saw it as his duty to build bridges between peoples

After celebrating Mass in the chapel of the Vatican's guest house with Vatican staff, the Pope takes a seat in the rear of the congregation to make his prayer of thanksgiving.

of different beliefs. "I really hope that the dialogue among us will help to build bridges to all people," he said, "so that everyone will see in the other not a rival, but a brother to accept and embrace." However he sounded another note of caution: "It is not possible to build bridges between people while forgetting God," he said. "But the converse is also true: it is not possible to establish true links with God, while ignoring other people."

Pope and predecessor

With that address to the diplomatic corps, Francis had completed the formal introductory meetings that any new Pope must schedule in the early days of his pontificate. But there was one important meeting still on his agenda, and it was one that no other pope in the past 700 years could even have contemplated: a private conversation with Benedict XVI.

In 1294, an encounter between St. Celestine V and his successor, Boniface VIII, had an unpleasant outcome: Boniface had Celestine imprisoned. Expectations were far more favorable for this meeting. By the end of his first week in office, Francis had enjoyed at least two friendly telephone conversations with Benedict, and he had spoken of his admiration for the retired pontiff at nearly

every opportunity. There was no doubt that the meeting would be cordial. But what else could the world expect?

"This is not a summit meeting between two leaders," a Vatican statement reminded journalists. Nor would there be any discussion of sharing responsibilities. There could be only one Pope; Benedict XVI had voluntarily given up his authority. The papal spokesman, Father Federico Lombardi, also dismissed a rumor that Benedict would give Francis a 300-page dossier of notes and advice about the problems of the Vatican.

Pope Francis made the trip to Castel Gandolfo on Saturday, March 23. Pope Emeritus Benedict—who appeared noticeably more frail than he had been just a few weeks earlier, when he took his leave of the Vatican—met him at the heliport on the grounds of the estate, and the two embraced warmly. They then went together to the chapel of the papal residence for a few minutes of prayer. As they entered the chapel, Benedict indicated to Francis that he, the reigning Pope, should take the place of honor in the front pew. Pope Francis declined. "We are brothers," he told Benedict, and he drew the older man up to kneel beside him.

From the chapel the two moved into the library, where they spoke privately for 45 minutes before joining a few aides for

lunch. The Vatican disclosed nothing about what they had discussed; Father Lombardi allowed only that it had been "a moment of profound communion" between the past and present popes. After lunch, Francis returned by helicopter to the Vatican.

Following the unprecedented meeting, the Vatican revealed that Pope Francis had brought a particularly significant gift for his predecessor. Three days earlier, the new Pope had received a Marian icon as a gift from Patriarch Kirill, the leader of the Russian Orthodox Church. Now the Pope passed that icon along to Benedict XVI. When he had received the icon, and been told that it was an image of "Our Lady of Humility," Francis told Benedict, "I immediately thought of you."

Benedict XVI was delighted by the gift, the Vatican reported. When he was informed that the icon he had presented to Pope Francis on behalf of the Russian Patriarch had been passed along so quickly, Metropolitan Hilarion, the chief ecumenical-affairs official of the Moscow Patriarchate, said that he was "very pleased and touched."

Francis and Benedict in prayer, side by side, in the chapel of the papal summer residence.

As a sign of reverence for the Pope Emeritus, Pope Francis presents Benedict XVI with an icon of Our Lady of Humility, a gift that had been presented to him by the Russian Orthodox Church.

St. Francis and the Franciscans

St. Francis of Assisi is one of the most beloved of all Catholic saints. The son of a wealthy cloth merchant, he was born around 1181. A carefree life ended when he was taken captive after a battle at Perugia, and spent more than a year in captivity. During that time he carefully examined his own life and experienced a profound religious conversion.

According to popular accounts, shortly after his release the young Francis dramatized his renunciation of worldly wealth by tearing off his rich clothes. Together with a few spirited companions, he began traveling around the region, clothed in simple robes, preaching and caring for the sick and the needy. The Franciscans held no possessions; they relied entirely on alms to support themselves and their work. In 1210, Pope Innocent III confirmed their right to preach and approved the first rules of their religious order.

The *Poverello* ("little poor man") quickly attained a wide reputation for sanctity, and became the focus of countless stories—including the legend that he preached the Gospel to the birds. As he acquired more followers, in 1211 he established several small monasteries. The following year, St. Clare of Assisi joined his movement, stablishing the Poor Clares for women.

The "troubadour of God" expanded his influence on preaching missions to Spain, southern France, and the Holy Land, where he tried to convert Muslim leaders to the Christian faith. But meanwhile divisions appeared within the Franciscan order. St. Francis was forced to relinquish leadership of the religious order he had founded.

St. Francis of Assisi. Fresco by Cimabue, Assisi monastery, circa 1278.

In 1224, after a 40-day fast on Mount La Verna, St. Francis received the stigmata: the wounds of Jesus appeared on his hands, feet, and side. Two years later, exhausted and nearly blind, he died at the Portiuncula monastery on the outskirts of his native Assisi. His reputation was so great that he was canonized, to popular acclaim, just two years after his death.

St. Francis is credited with popularizing the Christmas crèche. His songs—including the famous "Canticle of the Sun", are among the earliest surviving poems in the Italian vernacular.

Pope Francis makes his way in the 'popemobile' through a sea of admirers before Mass on Palm Sunday.

Dialog with Islam will
be one of the themes
of this papacy.

Challenges

Great things are expected of Pope Francis. Entering the conclave in which they selected him, the cardinals were hoping to find a pontiff who could reform the Roman Curia, present a revitalized perspective on Catholicism to an often hostile world, and inspire more than 1 billion members of an increasingly diverse global Church. At least at the start of his pontificate he would be frequently compared with a predecessor who was still alive: a challenge no other modern pope had faced. Will Francis be the Pope who finally travels to Russia, or to China? Will he visit war-torn Baghdad? Or will he concentrate on building up the faith in his own Rome diocese, and cleaning up the problems inside the Vatican?

The crisis of faith

Before Francis was elected, the Italian daily *La Stampa* listed five "unresolved issues" that a new Pope would need to address: the worldwide crisis of faith, the "reform of the reform" in the liturgy, the drive toward reconciliation with the breakaway traditionalist group the Society of St. Pius X, the reform of the Roman Curia, and the role of women in the Church. Actually that list of challenges was far too short, reflecting on the parochial interests of the Italian newspaper's editors. A more complete list would surely include the breakdown of the family, the bid for closer ties and ultimately full reunion with the Orthodox churches, the fight against persecution of Christians, the shortage of priests in the Western world (and accompanying questions about the tradition of clerical celibacy), the threats from militant Islam, the phenomenon of massive human migration, and the quest for real religious freedom. And yet the list would still be incomplete if it did not include the issue that Pope Francis quickly brought to the fore: the moral imperative to serve the needs of the poor.

During the pontificate of Benedict XVI, the top priority on the Vatican agenda was the crisis of faith, especially in the Western world. When he was elected to the papacy in 2005, Joseph Ratzinger chose to be known as Benedict, after St. Benedict of Nursia, whose religious order (the Benedictines) spread across Europe like wildfire in the 6th century, bringing order to a chaotic society and establishing the European identity that came to be known as Christendom. Pope Benedict's fondest aspiration was to spark another wave of Christian renewal, especially in the same European region, through the project he called the New Evangelization.

But Benedict's project faced entrenched opposition in Europe (and North America, also a prime target of the New Evangelization), where a thoroughly secularized society insisted that the Church could only prosper by changing its message. The Church was out of step with the 21st-century world, analysts said, because it condemned birth control and same-sex marriage, because it clung to the tradition of clerical celibacy and refused to ordain women as priests. Rome was keenly aware of these calls for change, and signaled a willingness to discuss changes that would not alter the fundamentals of Catholic doctrine. Pope Benedict frequently expressed his sympathy for couples who, because they were divorced and remarried, could not receive Communion. In *Light of the World* he allowed for the possibility that in some extreme cases—in relationships in which one partner was HIV-positive—the use of condoms might be justifiable. Cardinal Walter Kasper proposed allowing women to function as deacons—although he added that there would be no chance of altering the all-male priesthood, "the unbroken tradition of the Eastern Church as well as the Western Church."

Many bishops allowed that while the ordination of women was impossible, the discipline of priestly celibacy was not a matter of doctrine and could be changed. Then-Cardinal Bergoglio, for instance, was willing to discuss an end to the celibacy requirement. But he cautioned that he was "not sure its abolition would lead to an increase in vocations to the priesthood." The Argentine cardinal was not afraid of imposing high standards on candidates for the priesthood; he accepted only 40 percent of the candidates who applied to the seminary in Buenos Aires, screening all applicants carefully and setting the entrance standards unusually high. In *El Jesuita* he explained the rationale for celibacy, pointing out that a married priest has family commitments that make it impossible for him to dedicate himself entirely to ministry. Celibacy is not easy for a priest, the future Pope conceded. "It is a cross to bear and a new opportunity to strengthen his decision for God." He even

In the living and working areas of the papal apartments—sealed during the Conclave—numerous tasks await Francis, even if he decided not to live there.

expressed sympathy for priests who violated their vows, fathered a child, and then felt responsible for providing a home for that child; the cardinal said that he would be "the first person to support a priest in such a situation." But he would not tolerate clandestine romances. "What I will not permit," he said, "is living a double life."

Despite the ardent wishes of secular commentators—who observed with apparent surprise that Pope Francis was "conservative" because he upheld the enduring doctrines of the Church—there will be no fundamental changes in Church teaching under Pope Francis. The new Pope was not known for compromising on controversial moral teachings during his tenure as Archbishop of Buenos Aires. The Christian understanding of marriage and family life is close to his heart, and his unswerving commitment to uphold that model was evident in his vigorous campaign against legal abortion and same-sex marriage in Argentina.

"I really believe," Cardinal Bergoglio told an interviewer, "that the basic choice for the Church today is not to ease or eliminate rules, or to facilitate this or that, but to take to the streets and to seek out the people, getting to know them on a first-name basis." The approach known as "cafeteria Catholicism," in which believers pick and choose the Church teachings they will accept, is doomed to failure, he said. "This is a trend that has to do with consumerism," the Argentine prelate observed; people call for a lowering of moral standards "to justify the fact that they do not adhere to them." It would be sad, he said, to find that the calls for radical change in Catholic doctrine "ultimately expressed the absence of a personal encounter with God."

> "Yet Christ—not the successor of St. Peter—remains the center."
>
> *Pope Francis addressing representatives of the media on March 16, 2013*

So while leading prelates were willing to listen to the demands from secular opinion leaders in the West, and in fact anxious to show that they were listening, ultimately they set other priorities. Many Church leaders pointed to the Protestant denominations that had acceded to the same sorts of demands, bowing to contemporary trends. Those Christian communities were in much deeper trouble than the Catholic Church, Vatican prelates remarked; their churches were emptying. The Catholic Church, on the other hand, has persevered for over 2000 years largely because it has proven consistent in its teaching. Indeed the calls for dramatic change in Catholic teaching were now coming from exactly those places, in Europe and North America, where the faith was losing followers.

Thus the crisis of faith had been the Vatican's top priority. Pope Francis would have to decide how to continue with the Year of Faith proclaimed by Pope Benedict, which began on October 11, 2012, the 50th anniversary of the opening of Vatican II, and would continue until November 24, 2013 the feast of Christ the King. Both the Vatican and dioceses all over the world had launched hundreds of initiatives to stimulate knowledge of the faith and programs of evangelization. The programs were already in place, but the Catholic world would still be looking to the new pontiff for direction. Would the focus shift? Would the emphasis be changed?

Pope Francis seized an early opportunity to say that he fully intended to follow through with the project that Benedict XVI had begun. Ordinarily the Pope holds a public audience every Wednesday, but because of the swirl of activities between his election and his inauguration, Francis was not available for the midday audience until March 27—and that was Wednesday of Holy Week, with the Easter Triduum looming in the next few days. The Pope spoke at that audience on the meaning of Holy Week, the Passion and

Resurrection. But he assured the crowd in St. Peter's Square that on the following Wednesday he would resume the series of talks that his predecessor had begun, on the general theme of the Year of Faith.

A Catholic Action—torchlight march commemorating the 50th anniversary of the opening of Vatican II.

The Council and Continuity

Closely intertwined with the Year of Faith is the commemoration of the Second Vatican Council, which began 50 years ago. Pope Benedict XVI was one of the dwindling number of living witnesses to that important ecclesiastical event; he had attended the Council as a theological adviser to Cardinal Joseph Frings of Cologne, and had participated in the debates. With his departure, the papacy had undergone a noteworthy generational shift. Jorge Mario Bergoglio was a young student when the Council began. Benedict was surely the last Roman pontiff who had participated in the Council discussions; Francis was the first who was ordained after the Council.

While he highlighted the value and teaching authority of the Council, however, Benedict had insisted throughout his pontificate that teachings of the Council must be understood properly. He often denounced the many false interpretations of the Council, the "council of the media" that distorted Vatican II documents, the erroneous "spirit of the Council" that pulled in a direction opposite the actual written teachings of Vatican II. Shortly after his papal election Pope Benedict had delivered a stinging indictment of what he called the "hermeneutic of rupture"—the tendency to see Vatican II as a sharp break with the prior traditions of Catholicism. The antidote, he said, was an appreciation for

Tarcisio Bertone, the previous Cardinal Secretary of State, like all high Curia leaders was provisionally confirmed in his role.

continuity. Church doctrines do not change, he said, and therefore the teachings of Vatican II must be interpreted in the steady light of previous Church teachings. The Council was no break with the Catholic tradition, Benedict taught; Vatican II represented a development of Church teachings, in continuity with what had gone before.

That approach to the understanding of Vatican II disappointed some Catholics on both ends of the ideological spectrum: liberals who earnestly hoped for a complete break from the Catholic past, and conservatives who saw the Council as an unfortunate aberration that should be renounced. "The world experienced the Council through the eyes of the media," the German pope lamented, and the media had promoted the idea that any tenet of Christian dogma could be amended, submitted to popular vote, or thoroughly revamped without regard to the constant traditions

of Church teaching. The result, Benedict said, was a period of confusion and disorientation in Catholic life, with disastrous consequences: "closed seminaries, closed monasteries, trivialized liturgies."

During his days in Buenos Aires, Cardinal Bergoglio came to share some of Pope Benedict's negative appraisals of the changes that had swept through the Catholic world since Vatican II. As a Jesuit provincial he had seen some of his brothers seduced by Marxist ideology, while others grew disenchanted and left the priesthood and the Church. Yet at the major meetings of the Latin American bishops, Cardinal Bergoglio pressed for action to realize the vision of the Council. He was unusually active in his outreach to Christians of other faiths, to the local Jewish community, and to unbelievers. And he especially endorsed the "preferential option for the poor," which he described as "a strong message of the post-conciliar period."

The bishops' Synod

The Latin American bishops have joined in an uniquely strong continental body, the Episcopal Conference of Latin America (CELAM), which could furnish a model for the realization of another goal of Vatican II: the establishment of an active and influential worldwide Synod of Bishops. Pope Francis is no stranger to regular meetings of the worldwide Synod; he delivered one of the major addresses at the Synod of 2001. But his experience with CELAM could prompt him to strive for a different way of going about the Synod's work.

At the CELAM meeting in Argentina in 2007, Cardinal Bergoglio reports, "The work progressed from the foundation to the top, and not the other way around." He explained: "It was perhaps the first time that one of our general assemblies wasn't based on a pre-arranged text, but based instead on open dialogue." During the CELAM sessions every bishop had an opportunity to "openly speak his mind," and when the time came for the conference to vote on proposals, there were 2,240 suggestions to be weighed. The process was unwieldy but the results were impressive. "Our guideline was to include everything that came from the foundation, from the People of God," Cardinal Bergoglio said. "We didn't strive for synthesis; we strove for harmony."

It is scarcely imaginable that a meeting of the Synod of Bishops would convene without a text prepared in advance, or accept every good suggestion that was offered. Vatican meetings of the Synod have always been focused on a single, concrete topic (the Bible, the New Evangelization, the Liturgy, the Church in Asia or in Africa). The discussion revolves around a text that is prepared well in advance by the Vatican's office for the Synod, through a laborious process that involves circulating questions to all the world's bishops,

The Brazilian Franciscan Cardinal Cláudio Hummes, friend and confidante of Pope Francis.

preparing a draft statement in response to their replies, circulating that draft for further suggested amendments, and finally cobbling the results into a working document for the Synod's deliberations. The Vatican releases only short summaries of the topics that have been discussed in the Synod's closed sessions. So the world can gain a vague picture of the proceedings only through interviewers that reporters arrange with participating bishops.

There was one occasion, however, when a handful of journalistic observers, all from Vatican Radio, were allowed to observe the deliberations of a Synod meeting: a session in 2010, devoted to the Church in the Middle East. Those of

A group of Latin American bishops arrive at Managua's Cathedral in Nicaragua, May 12, 2009, to inaugurate with a Mass the 32nd Plenary Assembly of the Latin American Episcopal Conference (CELAM) in which they would discuss, among other issues, the missions in Latin America.

us who participated—dressed in somber colors, with neckties for men and covered shoulders for women—were deeply impressed by the experience. A Synod is not an open Council, but it can provide a truly surprising opening for dialogue among Church leaders. The wide diversity of the worldwide Church was visible, both in the identity of the participants and in the range of topics they chose.

For observers the experience was fascinating but confusing. Each speaker offered his own thoughts, usually without reference to those of the speaker before him. At the suggestion of Pope Benedict there were open, free-wheeling discussions at several evening sessions, and these generated some serious debates. In one instance there was even an angry confrontation between two bishops. For the journalistic observers the scene was intoxicating—

but also frustrating, because we were not allowed to report what we had seen and heard. There were open debates taking place inside the Vatican, and no one in the outside world would hear about them!

Therein lies the problem with the Synod: there is not (yet) a culture of open discussion and debate among the leaders of the Catholic Church, and especially among the officials of the Holy See. Could that change under the leadership of the Pope who saw the productive results of open debate in CELAM?

The butler did it

The need for a cooperative, collegial approach to the work of the Church is evident not just in the deliberations of the Synod but also, and especially, in the everyday work at the Vatican. The last major reform of the Roman Curia was undertaken by Pope Paul VI. During his long pontificate Pope John Paul II had other priorities; in his one major document on Vatican governance, *Pastor Bonus* in 1988, he essentially confirmed Pope Paul's reforms and even enhanced the broad authority of the Secretariat of State, which he described as the office "closest to the Sovereign pontiff." Curial reform was never one of Pope Benedict's main interests.

Although the Vatican has become a more international body, and there is much more geographical diversity now at the

Rio de Janeiro—Brazil, which hosts World Youth Day, July 2013, greeting a Pope from South America.

top level of administration, the Curia as a whole remains a predominantly Italian institution. The prefects of congregations and presidents of pontifical councils come and go, but they work with the same staffs, composed mainly of Italian veterans of Vatican affairs. The responsibilities of different offices are not precisely defined, and so conflicts and duplication of efforts are common. Only rarely has the pontiff sat down with Curial leaders for "cabinet meetings" to coordinate policies. There is no system of checks and balances to guard against the possibility that officials will head off in their own unproductive directions.

In the eight years of Benedict's pontificate, a steady stream of mishaps and scandals made it unmistakably clear that the work of the Curia was not proceeding smoothly. The Pope was not informed that a traditionalist bishop, whose excommunication he lifted, had denied the severity of the Holocaust. The man who was appointed head of the Vatican bank, with a mandate to establish transparency and enact tough new regulations against money-laundering, was forced to resign. Perhaps most personally painful to Benedict XVI, the Pope's own valet stole confidential papal correspondence, which then appeared in the Italian press and eventually in book form. The valet, Paolo Gabriele, was discovered, arrested, and convicted by a Vatican tribunal, and a Church spokesman said that he had acted alone. But most Vatican journalists still harbor a suspicion that the full details of the "Vatileaks" affair have not come to light. The list of Vatican missteps was a long one, and the constant scrutiny of the international media ensured that each error became well known.

The stories about internal mismanagement aggravated the damage already done by the sex-abuse scandal, which had subjected the world's entire Catholic hierarchy to critical scrutiny. Pope Benedict had resisted the temptation—to which some Vatican officials succumbed—to treat the scandal as an artifical problem created by the media. On the contrary, the Pope had sounded the alarm about the severity of the scandal, saying that the most devastating attack on the Church arose from "the sin within." He spoke of the "filth" within the Church, and cited the vision of St. Hildegard of Bingen, who saw the Church as a woman whose face was dirty and her clothes torn, defiled by the sins of her priests. During his pontificate he did his utmost to cope directly with the scandal, and to replace bishops who had covered up the crimes of their priests. He met a dozen times with victims of abuse, endured their bitter reproaches, and prayed with them—out of sight of the television cameras. He passionately exhorted the leaders of local churches in affected countries—notably Ireland—to repent, do public penance, and improve safeguards against abuse. Under his direction the Congregation for the

> "Dear brother Cardinals, this meeting of ours is intended to be, as it were, a prolongation of the intense ecclesial communion we have experienced during this period. Inspired by a profound sense of responsibility and supported by a great love for Christ and for the Church, we have prayed together, fraternally sharing our feelings, our experiences and reflections. In this atmosphere of great warmth we have come to know one another better in a climate of mutual openness; and this is good, because we are brothers."
>
> *Pope Francis to cardinals, March 16*

Doctrine of the Faith put pressure on the world's episcopal conferences to rewrite their own policies, setting higher standards.

Nevertheless the damaging effects of the scandal remain. In Rome, unflagging investigation of the handling of sex-abuse complaints uncovered evidence that some officials of the Roman Curia had fostered a culture of silence, protecting abusive priests and their diocesan leaders at the expense of innocent children and their unsuspecting families. These revelations played into the belief that there was corruption as well as incompetence within the Curia. The new pope would have to drive home the message to all Vatican officials that only honesty—not concealment, not hypocrisy—serves the true needs of Christ's Church.

The two most important offices of the Roman Curia are the Congregation for the Doctrine of the Faith (CDF), located in a building just to the left of St. Peter's Square, and the Secretariat of State, with offices in the apostolic palace. The Secretariat of State is not merely a foreign-affairs office, like the Department of State in the

U.S. or the Foreign Office in Great Britain. The Secretary of State is roughly equivalent to a prime minister; his office supervises the work of all the other Vatican offices (save only the CDF). Within the Secretariat of State there are two departments: one for foreign affairs, the other for internal Vatican business. The under-secretary in charge of the latter department, know as the *sostituto*, oversees all of the daily paperwork that flows through the Roman Curia.

Not only Assisi waits to greet the Pope.

Because the Secretariat of State combines diplomacy with internal Church work, Pope Benedict took a radical step when he appointed the former secretary of the CDF, Cardinal Tarcisio Bertone—a man with no experience in Vatican diplomacy—as his Secretary of State. The choice was unpopular among some curial officials. (According to persistent rumors, one such official was the prelate he replaced, Cardinal Angelo Sodano.) Criticism of Cardinal Bertone mounted as the list of Vatican gaffes lengthened, but Pope Benedict was steadfast in his support for his right-hand man. Cardinal Joachim Meisner of Cologne has frankly reported that after one particularly damaging debacle, he had spoken to the Pope on behalf of several other cardinals, urging him to dismiss Cardinal Bertone. The German cardinal said that the Pope was adamant: "Bertone stays! *Basta!*" ("Enough!")

To this day, many informed Catholics—and more than a few ranking prelates—believe that Pope Benedict resigned because he found himself unable to control the infighting among cliques within the Vatican. The aging Pope did not have the energy to handle the burden of work by himself, according to this theory, and he did not have the confidence in his staff that would allow him to delegate tasks. The *Frankfurter Allgemeine* theorized: "Benedict did not want to end up a marionette."

The Spanish Cardinal Julian Herranz, the chairman of the ad hoc committee set up by Pope Benedict to investigate the "Vatileaks" affair, disagrees with this theory. The Vatican, he told the newspaper *El Pais*, has the "least corrupt and most transparent administration" to be found, the cardinal said, and the "Vatileaks" scandal was "a bubble that burst on its own." But his is a minority opinion. The demand for reform of the Curia played a pivotal role in the conclave that chose Pope Francis, and he will be expected to address the problem quickly. His old friend, Cardinal Claudio Hummes, expressed confidence that Francis would tackle the challenge, but said that any reforms would be undertaken with a "spirit of simplicity, with a focus on the essentials."

In whatever he undertakes, Pope Francis will be watched by his silent German predecessor. This

St. Peter's Basilica and Square.

have no question that the former Pope plans to withdraw from public affairs—in effect to disappear. He will not be questioning his successor's policies or plans; he will not offer advice unless it is solicited. But his mere presence could tempt some factions within the Church to draw invidious

is an unprecedented situation. Despite the fact that Benedict pledged his unconditional obedience and support to his successor, the mere presence of the former pontiff poses new questions.

Eventually, once renovations are completed there, Benedict intends to move into a former monastery building in the Vatican Gardens. There the former Pope Benedict might easily encounter the former Cardinal Bergoglio on a morning walk. For Vatican officials, the prospect of having two popes at the Vatican was difficult to digest. It was hard to imagine that Benedict, who had lived in quiet splendor in the apostolic palace, would soon reside in this humble building below the Vatican Radio broadcasting tower.

Those who know Joseph Ratzinger best

comparisons, to wonder whether the policies of Francis would meet favor with Benedict. "I will advise Benedict at the earliest opportunity not to let himself be used by anyone," Cardinal Walter Kasper told the daily *La Repubblica*. But if the Pope Emeritus is committed to silence, and if any statement—even a rebuke to some faction—could be seen as intervention in the affairs of the current Pope, that advice will be difficult to carry out.

Ancient churches facing extinction

As Pope, Francis will be seen by Christians and non-Christians as the world's foremost spokesman for the Christian faith—a role that was strengthened by Pope John Paul II in his dozens of trips abroad. That leadership role carries a heavy responsibility in the early years of the 21st century, when Christianity is the world's most heavily persecuted faith.

Especially in countries ruled by Islamic law, Christians are at a disadvantage, legally treated as second-class citizens and sometimes subject to violence and intimidation. Many Christians, especially young families, have opted to emigrate to Europe or the Americas, seeking greater opportunities. The continual exodus of Christians has led to the near-extinction of the faith in some of the world's most ancient Christian communities, such as the Chaldeans of Iraq. Christians are even fleeing from the Holy Land, where the faith was formed. The universal Church faces the painful prospect that if these trends are not reversed, in the foreseeable future

Julian Cardinal Herranz, chairman of Benedict XVI's ad hoc commission to investigate the "Vatileaks" scandal.

only stones and ruins will testify to the faith in the region where Jesus lived.

Pope Benedict traveled to the Middle East several times, and with a special meeting of the Synod in 2010—shortly before the emergence of the "Arab Spring"—he attempted to rally a Christian revival in the Arab world. But he did not find a way to stop the steady bleeding of Christian emigration. The economic miseries and political insecurity that Christians face in the region are aggravated by the lack of unity among the diverse Christian bodies, which have often been more interested in protecting their own turf than in working together for the common good. Christian minorities in countries like Iraq and Syria have sometimes found temporary shelter from the political storms by attaching themselves to political parties that granted them some protection. But when political changes have come, and those parties have been ousted, Christians—now seen as allies of the former regime—have paid a heavy price.

It would be unreasonable to expect a Roman pontiff to resolve the deep-seated problems of instability in the Middle East, which have festered for hundred of years. Popes Paul VI, John Paul II, and Benedict XVI all traveled to the region. Papal trips cannot erase age-old animosities, but they can help to bring important topics to the forefront of international discussions, and they can help to improve the public understanding of Christianity in the countries visited. When

Pope Francis leads the Way of the Cross on Good Friday, March 29, 2013 at the Colosseum in Rome. The readings and special intentions focused on Christians who are persecuted for practicing their faith, especially in the Middle East.

Pope Benedict traveled to Turkey in 2006, at a time when the Islamic world was still in an uproar about his Regensburg address, 15,000 people demonstrated in Istanbul to oppose his visit, and armored tanks were lined up in front of the buildings where he would stay. But when the Pope arrived, the Turkish public saw a friendly, elderly man, not a hateful threat. "A congenial Pope," according to the newspaper *Hürriyet*, he became the subject of popular curiosity; the people of Turkey wanted to know more about this man and his faith. "The Pope should travel to a Mideast country every year," remarked a journalist from Libya. "He could achieve so much!"

When Pope Benedict traveled to Lebanon in 2012, the country's warring factions secretly agreed to a truce during the visit. As the papal motorcade passed through a district controlled by the Hezbollah faction, children waving Vatican flags lined the sidewalks. "For the first time we are seeing Lebanese flags hanging everywhere and not the posters of specific groups, militia or movements," commented Lebanese journalists. They were amazed to see feuding generals and politicians flocking together to the presidential palace to meet the pontiff and hear his discourse on religion and the quest for peace.

Pope Francis too will almost certainly want to travel to the Middle East: to the Holy Land, to make a pilgrimage and to contribute to the peace process there; perhaps to Istanbul, to pick up the thread of the conversation that was begun when Patriarch Bartholomew I came to Rome for his inaugural Mass; maybe to Egypt, where the "Arab Spring" took hold and where Coptic Christians are now endangered; possibly even to Baghdad or Damascus or even Tehran. During his tenure as Archbishop of Buenos Aires he showed that he has no great desire for international travel. But as leader of the universal Church he will find countless reasons—and countless invitations—to leave Rome.

Where the Church is growing

In all likelihood the first major international trip for Pope Francis will take him back to his own corner of the world, to the most Catholic of the world's continents: to Latin America. In July 2013, the international celebration of World Youth Day will take place in Brazil, a country where 65 percent of the population is Catholic. Pope Francis has already promised that he will be there. It seems logical to think that he would include a side trip to his native country. Indeed Francis has reportedly told several of his compatriots in Rome, "See you in Buenos Aires!"

There are 339 million Catholics in South America, and another 162 million in Central America. But there are vexing challenges for the Church in this Catholic bastion. Many of the region's Catholics are leaving the faith, to enter one of the many independent Christian churches that have proliferated in the region. Many Catholics who grow distant from their parishes gravitate toward the spontaneity, the emotion, and the immediacy of the faith preached in the Protestant groups. In 1996 the "free church" movement in Latin America claimed the affiliation of only 4 percent of the region's people; by 2010 that figure had jumped to 13 percent, and was still growing.

The Latin American hierarchy has been slow to respond to the exodus of Catholics. But CELAM has belatedly recognized the need for concerted evangelism adopting a "continental mission" to revive interest in the Catholic faith. For too long the Catholic hierarchy was usually identified with the privileged classes in a region marked by stark economic and social inequality; now the Church loudly proclaims its "preferential option for the poor." Catholic bishops have recognized that "base communities," in which several families join together for worship, can be instruments for evangelization as well as social action. While serving in Buenos Aires, Cardinal Bergoglio spoke of the need to welcome people warmly into parish life, and to go out into the streets to bring the Gospel to those who were not coming to church. He called for "a transformation of our structures, to become missionary."

If Catholic churches are suffering a loss of members in Latin America, they are experiencing vigorous growth in numbers in Africa: a continent that has seen the Catholic population soar by 21 percent in the last five years. If the trend continues, in just a few decades a majority of the world's Catholics will be African.

Yet even in Africa the Church faces some daunting challenges. The faith that missionaries brought to the continent often remained on the surface, not bringing fundamental changes to the people's way of thinking, not changing old ingrained habits of life. The Christian rule of monogamy has not yet taken firm root in African society; the discipline of clerical celibacy is frequently ignored. Independent preachers appeal to some Catholics in Africa, too, with their emotional appeals and claims to special powers of healing or ensuring success. Traces of indigenous superstitions are sometimes mixed into Catholic beliefs. The faithful clamor for liturgical practices that are more in keeping with their own cultural norms. Church leaders must steer a careful route, responding to their people's needs without sacrificing the accuracy of Church teaching and the reverence of Catholic liturgy.

Africa's myriad social and economic problems add to the Church's challenge. Hunger and poverty are commonplace, and Catholic charitable agencies struggle to cope with an overwhelming demand. The AIDS epidemic continues, and while Catholic institutions have been at the forefront in treating victims of

Dec 12, 2009: Faithful pilgrims of the Virgin during a procession to the Basilica of Guadalupe in Mexico City.

the disease, secular leaders have not accepted the Church's insistence that chastity and marital fidelity are the best means of prevention. Dictators sit ostentatiously in the front row at Sunday Mass—a phenomenon that will be familiar to Pope Francis after his experiences in Argentina. And Islam poses a growing threat in some countries, notably in Nigeria, where the terrorist group Boko Haram has mounted dozens of blood attacks on Christian churches.

In Asia, too, the Catholic Church is growing—by 11 percent in the past five years, second only to the rate of growth in booming Africa. But Christians remain a small minority on the world's most populous continent. If the Philippines, with their 81 percent Catholic population, did not color the continental statistics favorably, the picture would be bleak indeed. In China, in India, in Russia, Catholics make up less than 1 percent of the total population. Catholicism is generally viewed as a thoroughly foreign faith: an import from Europe. Nevertheless the dioceses and religious orders in many Asian countries maintain boarding schools, lay Catholics are socially active, and faithful play an important role in society, out of proportion to their tiny numerical representation.

A particular source of vexation for the Vatican is the quandary facing the Church in China, where the Beijing regime insists on control over the hierarchy and supports its own conference of bishops, unrecognized by Rome. Diplomatic relations between the Vatican and Beijing have been ruptured for decades, and under pressure from the regime the Catholic Church has been divided into two factions: the "official" Church that is approved and controlled by the government and the "underground" Church which suffers for its steadfast loyalty to the Holy See. In practice the dividing lines are frequently blurred; many of the bishops recognized by the Beijing government have sworn their allegiance to Rome, and most of the ordinary faithful are probably unaware of the struggles for control of their churches. At a time of the rapid transformation in Chinese society, Christianity exercises great appeal to millions of Chinese, and the number of Catholics is on the rise. The Beijing government is watching this growth uneasily, determined to keep the Church under the control of the Communist Party and persistently complaining about the Vatican's determination to "interfere" by appointing bishops. Clerics of the "underground" church are frequently harassed, intimidated, and sometimes imprisoned, especially if they challenge the right of the Communist Party to guide the hierarchy.

Demographic shifts

The historian of religion Philip Jenkins observed in the *New Republic* that every year more people are baptized as Catholics in the Philippines than in Spain, Italy, and France combined; there are more Catholics in metropolitan Manila today than in all of Holland. The Catholic Church, for centu-

Catholic prayer group in Africa.

ries perceived as a European institution, is now undeniably an international body, with its center of gravity shifting further to the global south. By the year 2030, if current trends continue, two-thirds of the world's Catholics will live in Latin America, Africa, and Asia: the continents once viewed as missionary territory. Jenkins wonders whether at some point the term "European Christian" will sound as incongruous as "Swedish Buddhist." The election of Pope Francis, the first pontiff from South America, helped to draw attention to this massive demographic shift.

Mass-goers receive a blessing to mark Palm Sunday outside a church in Quezon City, east of Manila, the Philippines March 24, 2013.

Still it is too early to write off European Catholicism. With 285 million faithful, the Church in Europe still rivals that in South America in size, although the European numbers are growing at an anemic 2 percent annual rate. There are 85 million Catholics in the U.S., and there the church membership is growing at a healthier 5 percent rate. On both sides of the northern Atlantic the Church has suffered a painful loss of credibility and prestige through the sex-abuse scandal. Moreover, in the most affluent Western countries the Church has been heavily engaged in a series of political battles: over abortion, same-sex marriage, euthanasia, stem-cell research, and similar emotional issues. From the perspective of secularists the Church has been on the wrong side of a large cultural shift. Even from the perspective of those who are not actively caught up in the culture battles, the Church risks being identified as a political interest group rather than a supernatural institution.

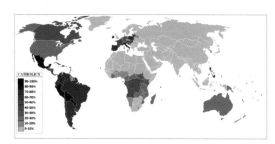

The Vatican will not simply accept the demise of the Catholic culture in Europe and North America. It was to revive the faith in these societies that Pope Benedict launched the New Evangelization, establishing a new pontifical council to coordinate the effort. In the fall of 2012 the Synod of Bishops centered its deliberations on the theme of this New Evangelization. Benedict XVI stepped down before writing the final document that would summarize the work of that Synod; that task now falls to Pope Francis. So the strategy paper explaining how the Church should revitalize the faith in Europe and North America will be written by a pontiff from neither region.

The decline of Catholicism in the Western world is certainly not irreversible. Five hundred years ago, much of Europe believed that the Catholic Church could not recover from the Reformation. "It not only survived, but grew stronger than ever in the long term," notes Philip Jenkins. The Catholic revival was due largely to new forms of popular piety and the formation of new groups dedicated to the unflagging promotion of the faith. Pope Francis is an enthusiastic supporter of popular piety, who personally practices the traditional devotions known for centuries by simple Catholic peasants. He is well acquainted with the new movements and small communities that have sprung up in Latin America to bring the Gospel to the people. The first non-European Pope in 1200 years may have the perspective needed to spur Europe's recovery of the Catholic faith today.